THE GROWTH OF CIVIL SOCIETY IN MYANMAR

Brian Heidel

THE GROWTH OF CIVIL SOCIETY IN MYANMAR

Published by
BOOKS *for* CHANGE
139, Richmond Road
Bangalore–560 025
Phone: +91-80–25580346
e-mail: bfc@actionaidindia.org
www.booksforchange.net

Edition: First, 2006

Price: Rs170.00 in India
        US$18.00 outside India

ISBN: 81-8291-023-4

B/C Production Team	:	Shoba Ramachandran, Rajeevan, Gokul and Shailaja
Design and Layout	:	Gokul, Rajeevan
Cover Design	:	Rajeevan

Contents

List of Tables

List of Graphs

Map

Acknowledgements

Many people have made this research possible. The dedicated team of researchers deserve special recognition for making this research possible despite very difficult circumstances. I would like to thank Martin Smith, David I. Steinberg, David Hulme and Ashley South for giving their valuable feedback on early ideas. I would also like to thank Caroline Marrs for reading drafts, providing valuable feedback and cleaning up the text. The insights of international NGO colleagues in Myanmar were very helpful. I am especially grateful to the front-line people, the local NGOs and CBOs for agreeing to participate in this unprecedented set of surveys and for openly sharing their views in one-on-one sessions and small-group discussions. Without their willingness to talk with me, my understanding would have been very limited. Finally, I would like to thank the many people in many communities who participated in the household survey.

Acronyms

BSPP	Burma Socialist Programme Party
CBO	Community-based organisation
INGO	International non-government organisation
MMCWA	Myanmar Maternal and Child Welfare Association
MRCS	Myanmar Red Cross Society
NGO	Non-government organisation
PTA	Parent Teachers Association
PPS	Probability Proportional to Size
SLORC	State Law and Order Restoration Council
SPDC	State Peace and Development Council
UN	United Nations
UNDP	United Nations Development Programme
UNICEF	United Nations Children's Fund
VPDC	Village Peace and Development Council
WHO	World Health Organization
YMBA	Young Men's Buddhist Association
YMCA	Young Men's Christian Association

1 Introduction

When was civil society born in Myanmar?[1] When did it die? Or did it never die?

"Civil society died under the Burma Socialist Programme Party (BSPP); perhaps, more accurately, it was murdered." (Steinberg 1999, p.8)

"It has been found that certain local organisations have been established by the non-government organisations to add efforts by the government organisations to carry out political, economic and social activities of the Union of Myanmar aiming to join hands with the people." (Ministry of Information 2002, p.241)

"... (T)he widespread belief outside Myanmar that there is no civil society in the country was never absolutely true and is even less so today (unless civil society is perceived in a strictly political sense)." (ICG 2002, p.25)

If civil society does exist in the country, are the organisations making up civil society independent and healthy? Are they free to operate?

"In fact, independent NGOs of the kind envisaged by international agencies have never become fully established [in Myanmar]." (Smith 1996, p.50)

"There is much more freedom than you can imagine, knowing this is a military government." (Interview with local NGO worker)

What are the prospects for civil society in the country?

"I wouldn't call it a bright future, but definitely it's progressing, moving forward." (Interview with international NGO worker)

"Overall, the prospect for the development of civil society in Burma is grim." (Liddell 1999, p.67)

People who care and comment on the nature of current-day civil society in Myanmar differ on many points. However, there is one point on which maybe everyone can agree. Civil society in Myanmar is poorly understood. In fact, the degree of confusion is phenomenal. Few countries today have such a poorly documented and networked civil society.

This research is the first of its kind inside the country, filling in many of the gaps of understanding civil society in Myanmar. The overall goal of the research is to increase understanding of the work of civil society organisations in ways that will improve interaction with those organisations and ultimately lead to meaningful changes in the lives of poor and marginalised people in Myanmar.

With the economy and social sectors in Myanmar showing signs of distress,[2] the state showing signs of retreat from the social sector,[3] and the international community beginning a gradual increase in attention and assistance,[4] all actors need to take a fresh look at how to support civil society actors in Myanmar, which are often neglected, or at best, poorly understood. It is likely that local civil society organisations could play an increasingly important role in addressing the basic needs and rights of people in Myanmar, both in short- and long-terms.

This research was carried out during 2003 and 2004, with two main surveys conducted over a period of eight months from April to November 2003. The bulk of the findings presented here revolve around these two main surveys. The first was a survey of

64 non-governmental organisations (NGOs), the second a survey of 455 community-based organisations (CBOs).

This paper consists of a chapter on NGOs in Myanmar, followed by a chapter on CBOs. In the conclusions section, recommendations are offered regarding the strengthening of Myanmar civil society. There are a number of annexes, including a detailed description of the research methodology.

Endnotes

1. This report uses the official name of the country. The country's name was Burma before 1989, and the name was officially changed to Myanmar in 1989. This report will refer to the country as Burma in reference to the pre-1989 period and Myanmar from 1989 onwards. This report follows the same practice for names of places in the country (e.g., Rangoon renamed Yangon). This is not meant as a political statement or endorsement of any particular group or ideology.

2. Many analysts believe that the Myanmar economy has stagnated for many years, and now lags far behind most other countries in the region (IMF 2002). Moreover, the UN ranks Myanmar 132 out of 177 countries in terms of human development (UNDP 2004).

3. Today less than US$0.60 per capita is spent annually on education and less than US$0.20 on health, one of the lowest levels of public investment in the world (UN/Myanmar Country Paper, February 2001, as cited in Taylor and Pedersen, 2005).

4. A number of bilateral donors and the EU have indicated possible increased humanitarian assistance to Myanmar in the coming years.

2 Background

A very brief summary of the evolution of civil society during the main periods of Myanmar's history.

Pre-colonial period

Going back centuries to the era of the Bagan and post-Bagan dynasties, civil society probably existed in some form. Most villages organised social events and welfare initiatives around the Buddhist temple. Monks led these events and initiatives, and a local organisation in most villages was formed to support the temple and related activities. The strong patronage system and hierarchy in society probably limited the number and type of organisations to very basic community-based social and religious groups. Yet there are records of many social and religious organisations within communities that were outside of direct state control.

The first recorded modern NGO was formed more than a century ago. The Burma Baptist Convention was formed in 1865.

British colonial period (1886–1948)

When the British invaded and established a colonial administration, they imposed and enforced many restrictions for the purpose of political/military control. Although controlling the population and limiting freedoms was a regular practice during the Burmese monarchy, the British were more effective in institutionalising control and limitations of freedoms (Furnivall 1960). These restrictions (limiting freedom of association, speech, movement and other rights) hampered the growth of civil society actors.

At the same time there was a contradictory trend. As educated urban Burmese growing up during the colonial administration were exposed to the practices of forming modern organisations and became more familiar with these practices, they showed a desire to create their own organisations for their own purposes, sometimes as a direct challenge to colonial control. For example, during the early part of the colonial administration, in 1906, the first modern, non-Christian NGO was formed – the Young Men's Buddhist Association. It began as a student group focusing mostly on religious topics, but later switched to emphasise political issues. They successfully led a campaign to ban footwear in all pagoda premises, using the opportunity to try to form an anti-colonial political movement. The origins of modern civil society were partially rooted in colonial resistance.

Post-independence 'democratic' period (1950s)

Following independence, civil society organisations began to multiply in urban areas. Many trade unions, professional associations and groups with a range of objectives were formed in the 1950s. (Steinberg 2001) NGOs and CBOs were apparently forming at a faster rate than at any other time in the country's history. This research attempted to collect information from the national library and other sources to document the formation and registration of organisations during this period. However, relevant documents were not made available, so further light could not be shed on this era.

BSPP period (1962–88)

With the coup in 1962 that brought General Ne Win to power, civil society was drastically changed. The military regime quickly imposed restrictions on many individual freedoms, and civil society organisations found themselves threatened. Local NGOs and CBOs retreated into a shell for several decades in order to survive. Some forms of civil society, such as labour unions and people's movements, were virtually wiped out. However, as this research illustrates, civil society survived and new organisations were forming continuously during this period, albeit at a much slower rate than before or after. And they adapted the way they function to the situation they faced.

Current period (1989–present)

During the SLORC/SPDC era, the government loosened some of the central controls on the economy and made attempts to encourage or tolerate foreign investment and foreign organisations to enter the country. A few international NGOs trickled into Myanmar in the early 1990s, and a larger flow entered in the late 1990s and first few years after 2000. Also, some of the severe restrictions on society appeared to soften somewhat, participatory forms of community organisation appeared to be more tolerated, and local and international NGOs were allowed to work at community level. In fact, many development workers have commented on the noticeably higher level of government tolerance at community level in Myanmar than in some other countries in Asia and elsewhere.

During this period, NGOs were also allowed increased access to sensitive border areas and to parts of the country where they could not previously work. The numerous ceasefire agreements signed between the SPDC and armed ethnic groups during the 1990s also contributed to increasing access for NGOs around the country.

3 NGOs in Myanmar

Definition and Selection of NGOs for the Survey

The seven main criteria used to define an NGO for the purposes of this survey were:

- non-profit;
- voluntary initiative;
- relative independence from political parties and organisations, and from government;
- self-governing;
- self-perception as accountable in some way to society;
- disinterest, in the sense of working on behalf of others and not their own staff, members or committees;
- socially progressive, that is, having at least one human development or social welfare aim.

Thus, while organisations like sporting associations were excluded, religious organisations were not excluded a priori. Out of this group of socially progressive NGOs, only organisations that were willing to participate in this study were included. In the end, nine NGOs that otherwise fit the research criteria declined to participate. Also, only those that could be reached were included.

(Representatives from one NGO that otherwise fit the criteria could not be located).[5] Finally, it is important to note that the research selected only those NGOs with an office or headquarters in the capital Yangon, regardless of where in the country the organisation implemented programmes. However, to be defined as an NGO, the organisation had to be operational in more than one distinct geographical area or serving beneficiaries from more than one geographical area (unlike CBOs, see the next chapter).

The research included as NGOs five somewhat specific organisations (bringing the total number surveyed to 64 organisations). These five organisations were part of the relatively large group of organisations which, while nominally non-governmental, were nevertheless officially recognised and sanctioned by the Government of Myanmar. (Many NGOs have legal recognition, but they do not have this same degree of official sanction). While other organisations in this group (which numbered 25 according to the Ministry of Information's latest official list from 2002, see Table 1), might otherwise have been included in the survey because of their social welfare aims, they were judged to be insufficiently independent of the government to be considered bona fide NGOs. Other organisations from this list simply did not meet the social welfare aim criterion.

Among these 64 organisations are 35 that can be considered 'institutional', providing subsidised services to people in homes, schools, and hospitals.

NGOs were asked to classify themselves. Table 3 shows that 40 NGOs (63%) defined themselves as religious in some way. The table also shows that 10 NGOs defined themselves as 'mass' organisations, a category generally understood in Myanmar to mean organisations with national scope, usually having branch offices in many, if not all, states and divisions of the country. Oftentimes such organisations aim to represent all representatives of a given group, such as youth or professionals in a single

Table 1

Organisations on the Ministry of Information's List of Social Organisations (2002)

Included in the NGO Survey	Not Included (no welfare aims)
Forest Resource Environment Development and Conservation Association	Foreign Correspondents Club of Myanmar
Myanmar Health Assistants Association	Myanmar Dental Association
Myanmar Medical Association	Myanmar Engineering Society
Myanmar Nurses Association	Myanmar Floriculturists Association
Myanmar Women's Entrepreneurs Association	Myanmar Hiking and Mountaineering Association
	Myanmar Library Association
Not included (not independent)	Myanmar Motion Picture Asiayone
Myanmar National Committee for Women's Affairs	Myanmar Music Asiayone
	Myanmar Photographic Society
Not included (not voluntary initiative)	Myanmar Printing and Publishing Association
Auxiliary Fire Brigade	Myanmar Sports Writers Federation
Myanmar Maternal and Child Welfare Association[6]	Myanmar Theatrical Asiayone
Myanmar Red Cross Society	Myanmar Traditional Artist and Artisans Asiayone
Myanmar War Veteran Organisation	Myanmar Writers and Journalists Association
	Union of Myanmar Chambers of Commerce and Industry

profession. While the term might be interpreted negatively by outsiders (meaning an organisation established by government for the primary purpose of extending its control over the population), it was apparently not seen as negative among NGOs in Myanmar.

Table 2

List of Surveyed NGOs*

1	All Myanmar Tamil Hindu Foundation
2	All-Myanmar Hindu Federation (Centre)
3	Asho Chin Baptist Conference
4	Catholic Bishops Conference of Myanmar
5	Dhamma Theikdhi Monastic Education School
6	Dhammaythaka Parahita Nunnery School
7	Eden Handicap Service Centre
8	Forest Resource Environment Development and Conservation Association
9	Funeral Help Organisation
10	Grace Home (Orphanage)
11	Guru Nanak Free Dispensary and Eye Hospital
12	Hman Kinn Monastic Education School
13	Hninzigone Home for the Aged
14	Jivitadana Sangha Hospital
15	Kachin Baptist Convention
16	Karuna Myanmar Social Services
17	Kayin Baptist Convention
18	Law Kahta Cariya Foundation
19	Little Sisters of the Poor Home for the Aged Poor
20	Madarsah Majidia Hifzul Quraan and Orphanage
21	Mary Chapman School for the Deaf
22	Metta Development Foundation
23	Mingalar Byu-har Welfare Association

24	Muslim Free Hospital And Medical Relief Society
25	Muslim Women's Home for the Aged
26	Myanmar Anti-Narcotics Association
27	Myanmar Baptist Convention (MBC)
28	Myanmar Business Coalition on AIDS
29	Myanmar Christian Fellowship of the Blind
30	Myanmar Christian Health Workers' Services Association
31	Myanmar Christian Leprosy Mission
32	Myanmar Health Assistant Association
33	Myanmar Literacy Resource Centre
34	Myanmar Nurses Association (Centre)
35	Myanmar Women Entrepreneurs' Association
36	Myanmar Women's Development Association
37	Myanmar Young Crusaders
38	Myitta Wadi Parahita Monastic Education School
39	Nan Oo Education and Parahita School
40	National Council of Young Men's Christian Associations
41	Ngapyaw Kyun Nunnery School
42	Patack Shwewar Monastic Primary School
43	Pwo Kayin Baptist Conference
44	Pyiññya Tazaung Association (Light of Education)
45	Sasana Rakkhita Buddhist Missionary Monastic Primary School
46	Shalom Foundation (Nyein Foundation)
47	Shwe Pyi Hein Free Health Services-on-Wheels
48	Shwe Thanlwin Home for the Aged
49	Tezeindarrama National Races Parahita School
50	The Myanmar Council of Churches
51	The Myanmar Medical Association
52	The Salvation Army - Myanmar Region
53	Three-Storey Parahita Monastic Education School

54	U Hla Tun Hospice (Cancer) Foundation
55	Wai-Naya Sukha Drinking Water Association
56	Yadana Beikman Parahita Monastic Education School
57	Yadanapon Yeik Nyein
58	Yangon Kayin Baptist Women Association
59	Yinthway Foundation
60	Young Men's Buddhist Association (YMBA)
61	Young Men's Christian Association Yangon
62	Young Women's Christian Association (National)
63	*Did not wish to be named*
64	*Did not wish to be named*

* *(except for two organisations that agreed to participate in the survey but did not wish to be identified).*

Possibly the single largest driving force for civil society initiatives around the country has been religion. Religious NGOs are not only more numerous than any other type of NGO, they are also much older. In fact, it was not until 6 decades after the first modern religious NGO was established that the first modern non-sectarian NGO was formed.

> *"The quintessential examples of civil society ubiquitous throughout Burmese history have been religious organisations at the local level."* (Steinberg 2001, p.105)

Each of the four major religions of Myanmar (Buddhism, Christianity, Islam and Hinduism) has made a unique and important contribution to social and economic development in the country. Many NGOs have formed out of each of the major religions. However, the data from this research clearly show that the number of Christian NGOs was much larger than the proportion of Christians in the population, while the number of Buddhist NGOs was much smaller. The number of Hindu and Muslim NGOs was closer to the population ratio for those religions. The scope of this research did not include an in-depth study of the role of religion and civil society. This topic would make an interesting study for future researchers. However, some observations can be made which might give a better understanding of this pattern.

Table 3

NGOs by Type

Type of NGO	Number	Percentage
Religious-affiliated organisation	28	44%
Other organisation	10	16%
Professional association	6	9%
Professional + Religious-affiliated organisation	4	6%
Professional + Other organisation	3	5%
Mass + Religious-affiliated organisation	3	5%
Mass organisation	3	5%
Mass + Religious-affiliated + Ethnic-based organisation	2	3%
Religious-affiliated + Other organisation	1	2%
Religious-affiliated + Ethnic-based organisation	1	2%
Mass + Religious-affiliated + Professional organisation	1	2%
Mass + Professional association	1	2%
Ethnic-based organisation	1	2%
Total	**64**	**100%**

Buddhist monks in Burma had a long history of organising movements against oppressive practices of the state. In response, activities of the 'Sangha' (order of Buddhist monks) have been limited through various recent laws, instructions and interventions. In 1980, following a purge of monks, the government organised a congregation of monks to produce the 'Fundamental Rules of Organisation of the Sangha', keeping tighter control of monks' activities. (Liddell 1999, pp.66–67)

During the research some Buddhist monks acknowledged that their orientation was not focused on poverty and suffering. Four decades ago one researcher noted the tendency for Buddhists in the country to focus strongly on gaining personal merit. He observed the 7 ways that Buddhists practised their faith in a rural village, and the last and least of those practices was related to assisting a fellow person with some type of charity. (Nash 1965, p.116)

Other aspects of religious organisations have caused some serious concerns among the international development community. The religious NGOs, who made up a majority, sometimes did not clearly separate their religious and social/developmental goals. However, a more encouraging development was the start of an inter-faith dialogue. Some religious communities were actively promoting joint efforts to reduce barriers and mistrust in conflict areas and increase better cooperation and understanding.

In the following sections, the findings of a comprehensive survey administered to these 64 NGOs are presented. The survey research was complemented by focus group discussions and key informant interviews with knowledgeable observers from international and UN organisations. These observations are included throughout the paper, in an attempt to add perspective to the survey findings.

NGO Formation

Though the research team did attempt to find information on all NGOs ever registered or active in Myanmar over the past 100 years, records on NGOs previously registered but no longer in existence were not available at the Ministry of Home Affairs. Therefore, it was not possible to identify all NGOs that were ever formed. Nevertheless, based on the dates the 64 surveyed NGOs were formed (please see Graph 1), some patterns emerged.

Graph 1. Formation of New NGOs by Decade

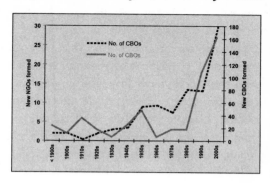

Aside from the fairly remarkable finding that NGOs formed over 100 years ago were still in operation during the survey period (2003), the pattern of NGO formation shows that during two decades – the 1950s and 1990s – there was a marked increase in NGO formation. These periods of relatively brisk NGO formation seem to correspond to the most likely periods in Myanmar's history in which such growth would have occurred. Thus, eight of the surveyed NGOs were formed during the relatively open 1950s (almost one per year) and 27[7] were formed during the current decade; that is, about three per year. In contrast, seven of the surveyed NGOs were formed during the 29-year BSPP era (from 1962–1988) or about one every 4 years, and 19 were formed during the 62-year period of the British colonial government (1886–1948), or about one every 3 years.[8] From 2000 to 2002 alone, nine NGOs were formed. Nevertheless, the median age of surveyed NGOs was 40 years. Again, it is important to remember that data do not capture NGOs formed in any of these periods that either no longer exist or that continue to operate but were not included in this survey.

Estimated Number of NGOs in Myanmar

Based on the number of NGOs identified in Yangon, the survey attempted to estimate the total number of NGOs in Myanmar. The 64 NGOs included in the NGO survey represented 100% of the known NGOs based in Yangon that met the research criteria and that were willing to participate in the survey. Adding the nine NGOs that probably met the research criteria but refused to participate, plus another estimated 10% that were missed, and another estimated 50% that met all research criteria except the one describing human welfare aims, the number of NGOs in Yangon would rise to 120. Based on the information available, this is a reasonable estimate for NGOs with head offices in Yangon. Outside Yangon, Mandalay most likely had the next largest concentration of NGOs. Based on observations, it can be estimated that Mandalay had about one-fourth the number of NGOs compared with Yangon. Therefore, Mandalay would have had an estimated 30 NGOs. Assuming for the purposes of this estimate that each of the remaining 12 states and divisions had ten NGOs each, the total number of NGOs in Myanmar would come to 270. This number cannot be verified, so it should be taken as a preliminary estimate until a better count can be taken.

Some studies have attempted to count all NGOs in selected countries and compare across countries. However, there are so many deficiencies and discrepancies that making any cross-country comparisons becomes almost meaningless (Fisher 1997). For example, if Myanmar had about 270 NGOs, it would fall far behind the Philippines (6,000 NGOs), in terms of overall numbers, but it would be a bit ahead of Thailand (200 NGOs). As another example, the 'density' of NGOs, given the estimated Myanmar population of approximately 52 million (CSO 2002), would be 5.2 per million, comparing rather favourably with a number of countries, albeit being below the global average (Fisher 1997). However, these comparisons are fraught with inconsistencies, as the formation, registration and counting of NGOs are vastly different across countries. Therefore, the only cross-country observation that can be made is that Myanmar civil society is not insignificant. Naturally, the quality and the health of civil society in Myanmar is another question altogether. This question will be addressed in the following sections.

NGO Legal Context

Less than half (29) of the NGOs reported being legally registered with the Government of Myanmar;[9] an additional 4 NGOs were currently in the process of seeking legal recognition. The fact that barely half of the surveyed NGOs were registered or seeking registration does not mean that the remaining NGOs were working 'underground'. (As reported earlier, only two of the 64 surveyed NGOs did not wish to be identified for this paper.) Rather, NGOs were either unaware of the need to register, or were daunted by complicated and time-consuming procedures to do so. However, 67% of the registered NGOs, or 19 NGOs reported that the process was not difficult. Indeed, these same NGOs reported that their waiting period was shorter than expected, averaging about 8 months. [10]

As part of this research, a legal review was conducted. Annexure B contains a more detailed overview of the findings from this review, focusing on the legal context in Myanmar for NGOs and CBOs, including a comparison of the different laws under which NGOs may register. (CBOs are not legally obliged to register, though some do.) As of 2004, there was no law specifically geared to non-profit organisations in Myanmar. However, the legal review revealed that the 1988 Organisation of Association Law was probably the most relevant for NGOs. Other registration laws applicable to NGOs included the Partnership Act (1932), the Cooperative Society Law (1992) and the Code of Civil Procedure (1908). Briefly, amongst the 29 NGOs that had registered, 22 (or 76%) did so under the Association Law. Four NGOs stated that they had registered under the Societies Registration Act (since annulled and replaced with the Association Law, bringing to 26 the surveyed NGOs registered under this law), and one registered under the Myanmar Companies Act (1955) which, according to this research, would not seem to be appropriate for an NGO. Two NGOs could not name the law under which they had registered.

Specific tax exemption status did not exist under Myanmar law, as of 2004. NGOs can achieve a de facto tax exemption by stating their charitable, non-profit purposes in their legal registration documents. As long as they operated without earning a profit, they were not obligated to file an income tax return. Given that NGOs did not, therefore, benefit from any explicit and specific tax exemption from the government, and yet did not pay taxes, it may be understandable that NGOs were confused on the issue of tax exemption. In the survey, 29 NGOs responded that they were exempt from taxes, 29 responded that they were not exempt, while the remaining six did not know. The degree of confusion was similar even for the 29 NGOs who reported being legally registered: fifteen of them said they were not tax exempt, eleven said they were, and three said they did not know.

NGO Geographical Reach

Table 4 shows where the 64 surveyed NGOs worked. Myanmar is divided into 14 states and divisions (see map). While these are comparable administratively, the main distinction is that divisions tend to be more uniformly ethnic (Bamar, who represent approximately 70% of the Myanmar population), while states have significant ethnic minority groups. The seven states of Kachin, Kayah,[11] Kayin,[12] Chin, Mon, Rakhine and Shan are around the country's perimeter, and the seven Divisions of Sagaing, Tanintharyi, Bago, Magway, Mandalay, Yangon and Ayeyarwady are in the interior and the perimeter. The next level of organisation is the District, followed by the Township (of which there are 324) village tract (rural) and ward (urban) levels. Annexure F contains a table showing Myanmar's total population (52 million) divided by State and Division.

Table 4

Number of Yangon-based NGOs, by State or Division

State or Division	Number of NGOs
Yangon Division	64
Mandalay Division	18
Bago Division	17
Ayeyarwady Division	17
Shan State	14
Kachin State	14
Mon State	13
Kayin State	10
Sagaing Division	8
Chin State	8
Magway Division	6
Kayah State	5
Rakhine State	4
Tanintharyi Division	3

Note: Yangon-based NGOs all work in Yangon (64); each of the 64 NGOs may in addition work in one or more of the other states or divisions in Myanmar.

As expected, all 64 NGOs had programming in Yangon. (This was almost inevitable, as the criterion for inclusion in the survey was for the NGO to have an office in Yangon). Many worked in more than one state or division. Eighteen (or 28%) of the surveyed NGOs worked in Mandalay, followed closely by Bago and Ayeyarwady divisions, with 17 NGOs each. States or divisions with the lowest level of Yangon-based NGO presence included Tanintharyi Division (3), Rakhine State (4) and Kayah State (5), which are remote and/or conflict-affected areas.[13] Divisions, excluding Yangon, had an average of about 12 NGOs working in them, while states had an average of about 10 NGOs.

NGO Sectors and Beneficiaries

NGOs were asked to report on all sectors in which they worked. Table 5 shows that half (32) of surveyed NGOs worked in the education sector. Sectors in which at least 20% of surveyed NGOs worked (that is, at least 12 NGOs or more) include, in order of importance, health (25 NGOs), religious affairs (22), social welfare (21), water and sanitation (15), HIV/AIDS (14) and agriculture (12).

Table 5

Number of NGOs by Sector

Sector	Number of NGOs
Education	32
Health	25
Religious	22
Social Welfare	21
Water and Sanitation	15
HIV/AIDS	14
Agriculture	12
Credit	11
Emergency	8
Environment	8
Other	8
Nutrition	7
General Capacity Building	6
Non-Violence, Conflict Resolution	1

Map of Myanmar

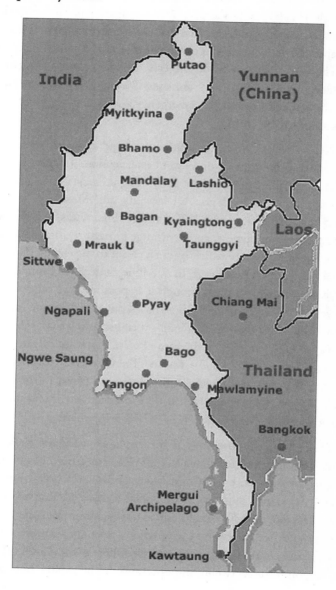

By funding allocation, NGOs reported that most of their programming funds went to health (19%), social welfare (12%), agriculture (11%) and education (7%). Comparing this information to Table 5 might indicate that NGOs were managing a small number of relatively large agriculture projects and a great number of relatively small education projects. Rounding out the sectors by allocation were water and sanitation (3%) and HIV/AIDS (2%); nutrition, conflict resolution, emergency and human rights all had allocations of 1% or less.

NGOs were also asked about the kind of work they did according to the state or division of intervention. Table 6 reveals a number of interesting points. After Yangon, most NGO activity was concentrated in Bago, Ayeyarwady and Mandalay (all of which are divisions, notably). Kachin and Shan states had, despite their relative remoteness, good coverage in most sectors, on a par with that of Mon state which is much closer to the capital. On the other hand, NGO coverage in Rakhine State and Tanintharyi Division was very limited though it is possible that other, non-surveyed NGOs (particularly those based outside of Yangon) might have been filling these gaps. Finally, it is interesting that only one surveyed NGO worked in the area of conflict resolution and this, in only one state, namely Kayin. There was a noteworthy concentration of HIV work in Bago division (third in the table after Yangon and Mandalay), a division that few international agencies focused on in their HIV/AIDS programming.

The table also shows how sector emphasis in Yangon could be quite different than in other places. While education, health and religious affairs were fairly consistent across the whole country, there was rather more focus on social welfare in Yangon than elsewhere (social welfare ranks fifth in importance in Yangon, while it is seventh for the country as a whole). Not surprisingly, there was greater emphasis on agriculture elsewhere in the country than in Yangon (it ranks twelfth in importance in the capital, but sixth for the country as a whole). Water and sanitation interventions appeared to be somewhat consistently spread across the country, including Yangon.

Table 6

NGO Activity by Location and by Sector

Location Sector	Education	Health	Religious Affairs	HIV/AIDS	Watsan	Agriculture	Social Welfare	Credit	Environment	Emergencies	Capacity Building	Other	Nutrition	Conflict Prevent.	Total
Ayeyarwaddy	9	6	8	4	6	7	4	5	4	4	2	1	0	0	60
Bago	9	8	7	7	7	5	3	7	4	3	2	2	0	0	64
Chin	2	2	3	1	4	2	1	1	1	0	1	0	0	0	18
Kachin	6	5	4	5	3	5	0	3	3	2	3	1	1	0	41
Kayah	1	2	1	1	1	1	0	1	1	1	2	0	1	0	13
Kayin	3	4	4	3	3	3	2	0	2	1	2	0	0	1	28
Magway	3	2	2	2	3	1	2	1	1	1	0	0	0	0	18
Mandalay	8	8	6	6	7	3	2	3	3	3	1	1	2	0	53
Mon	6	5	7	4	4	3	3	1	2	2	1	0	1	0	39
Rakhine	1	1	1	1	1	0	0	0	0	0	0	0	0	0	5
Sagaing	2	3	3	3	4	2	1	1	1	1	0	0	0	0	21
Shan	5	5	3	6	5	4	2	3	2	1	1	1	1	0	39
Tanintharyi	1	2	1	2	0	1	0	0	1	1	0	1	0	0	10
Yangon	27	21	22	12	8	3	18	5	5	3	6	7	5	0	142
Total	**83**	**74**	**72**	**57**	**56**	**40**	**38**	**31**	**30**	**23**	**21**	**14**	**11**	**1**	

NGOs were also asked to name the sectors in which they thought they might have the most impact in the future. NGOs named social welfare (42%) and health (36%). In the case of social welfare, this might mean that NGOs would like, or see opportunities to expand their significant social welfare activities in the capital to other parts of the country. In any case, it is somewhat surprising that education, currently the top sector in terms of numbers of NGOs, was named by only six NGOs. HIV/AIDS and water/sanitation were also mentioned rarely (1 mention each) in this regard.

With regard to beneficiaries, according to Table 7, the single most frequently mentioned primary beneficiary group was the 'general population', followed by poor communities, pre-school/school children and orphans. Given the high level of poverty in Myanmar, it is surprising that a minority of the responses listing primary beneficiaries (45%) could be classified as poor or marginalised people. (The remaining 55% could be described as general population.) It must be remembered that the surveyed NGOs were included in the research if they met the criteria, including having at least one activity or goal related to human welfare or human development. Unlike a sporting federation, for example, the surveyed NGOs would be expected to have a greater focus on poverty. A brief analysis of the NGOs' vision statements also found that they seldom mentioned poverty or poor and marginalised groups.

NGO Funding

NGOs as a whole were managing higher levels of funding than ever seen before in Myanmar. Nevertheless, annual budgets were quite small (under US$10,000) for almost half of NGOs. Graph 2 shows that the largest proportion (30%, or 19 NGOs) had annual budgets of less than US$3,272, while another 14% (or 9 NGOs) had budgets between US$3,720 and US$9,640. In the upper ranges, 6% (or 4 NGOs) had budgets of US$109,050 or higher.

Table 7

Types of Primary Beneficiaries Served by NGOs

Type of Primary Beneficiaries	Number of NGOs	Percentage
General population	19	31%
Poor communities	13	21%
Pre-school and school children	11	18%
Orphans and handicapped	11	18%
Poor children	10	16%
Communities of a particular region	10	16%
Women	7	11%
Poor elderly people	4	6%
Persons in poor health	4	6%
Persons affected by leprosy	2	3%
Communities affected by disasters	2	3%
Persons affected by HIV/AIDS	1	2%
Drug abused persons	1	2%
Illiterates	1	2%

NB: NGOs were allowed to name more than one type of beneficiary.

Of the 55 NGOs who provided budget information (as shown in the graph, 14%, or 9 NGOs elected not to answer budget questions), 45 elected to provide exact figures (the other 10 provided ranges instead). The total combined annual budget of the 45 NGOs who gave exact budget figures was the equivalent of approximately US$2 million. While the average budget was therefore about US$44,000, the range of annual budgets was quite wide: the smallest annual NGO budget was approximately US$440, while the largest was about US$500,000. With regard to the remaining ten NGOs that provided their budget information in ranges, taking the mid-point of each range as the estimated budget, the combined total of these 10 NGOs' budgets was US$123,900. The combined annual budget for 55 NGOs was approximately US$2.1 million. Therefore, the average annual budget of each NGO in Myanmar was US$38,300 in 2003.

Graph 2. Annual Budget Ranges of NGOs

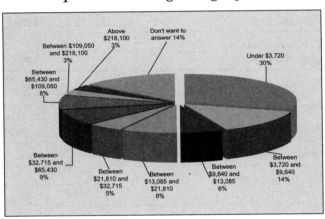

It is difficult to give an accurate picture of the sources of the funds provided for the NGOs surveyed because there were some apparent contradictions in the information collected from different sources. According to the information provided by the NGOs, UN agencies provided only a small fraction of their resources (2003 figures). International NGOs provided US$820,000 or 39% of the total amount; public donations amounted to a very significant US$704,000 (33%); religious institutions (9%); foreign governments (7%); the Myanmar government (1.0%); and, UN agencies (0.7%).

In sharp contrast to the figures provided by the surveyed NGOs, six of the seven UN agencies that funded NGOs (one agency did not fund NGOs at all) stated that they contributed US$2 million to NGOs in 2003 (representing 26% of their budgets, versus 36% given to the Government of Myanmar and 20% to INGOs). Amounts accorded to local organisations ranged from US$52,000 to US$1,300,000. On average, each of the six UN agencies provided US$339,687 to local NGOs in 2002.

Part of the apparent contradiction in the earlier two paragraphs is explained by the fact that the UN agencies provided funding for NGOs that were not represented in this research, like the Myanmar Maternal and Child Welfare Association and the Myanmar Red Cross Society. However, this does not explain all of the apparent discrepancies. It was subsequently confirmed that one UN agency disbursed a total of US$580,000 in 2003 to NGOs included in the study. This would indicate that some local NGOs did not reveal all of their funding sources in the survey.

A previous unpublished survey in 2001–02 conducted by a small group of INGOs found that only about 28% of the INGOs working in Myanmar were providing some funding to local organisations. However, it was not clear if the INGOs in that survey made a distinction between local NGOs and CBOs. The amounts they provided were relatively small (under $50,000) except 2 INGOs providing between $300,000 and $500,000. Comparing the 2002 survey with this research, it appears much of the funding is coming from INGOs based inside Myanmar but some is coming from outside.

Further complicating the picture, only 27 NGOs (42%) stated that they received funding from international donors. Of these, nine NGOs (or 33%) reported that it was difficult to raise funds from international donors, while 15 NGOs (56%) said it was not difficult (three NGOs said they did not know). When asked to compare fundraising from international donors currently (in 2003) to two years previously, 14 (52%) said it was more difficult currently, and ten (37%) said it was about the same. Only three NGOs (11%) said it was easier. This increased difficulty experienced by more than half of the NGOs receiving international donor funding is another worrying trend. The research could not independently assess whether or not donors' application procedures were excessively difficult.

In contrast, 46 NGOs (71%) received funds from a local source. The survey's follow-up question, which asked if fundraising from local sources was easier or more difficult currently, reveals that 35% found it easier currently, 22% found it more difficult and 43% saw no change (whether difficult or easy).

Overall, NGOs experienced much success in fund raising. Among the 16 NGOs that reported applying for grants from donors in the last fiscal year, the number of applications ranged from 1 to 14 per NGO (only three NGOs made more than three applications). Only two of the 16 NGOs reported having applications rejected, of which one was for a late submission. The other NGO had an overall success rate of 20% with grants. The other 12 NGOs were 100% successful, including one NGO that applied 14 times in the last year. In total, these NGOs were successful in 42 grant applications. Significantly, these NGOs reported managing exactly 42 projects in the past year. In other words, none of these NGOs was managing more grants than it had applied for and received last year. This might indicate that most grants accorded to NGOs were short term, probably not lasting longer than two years. Follow-up interviews with a sub-set of NGOs confirmed that sustainability and long-term planning were constrained by short-term funding. This was an unhealthy situation for NGOs.

Satisfaction with the amount of funding was mixed. Half of NGOs (32) did not find funding to be a constraint, while 44% reported that funding was a constraint for their NGO. Ninety-one per cent (58 NGOs) indicated they wanted to increase funding and believed they had the capacity to absorb an increase. Two of these NGOs chose not to answer subsequent questions, but amongst the 56 who did, eight felt they had the capacity to double or even triple their work, 23 NGOs said they had the capacity to expand between 50–99% of their current level of work, and 25 to expand their work anywhere from 10 to 49%. Most of these same NGOs, 43 in fact, did not believe there was any significant risk associated with expansion. For those that did (19), most of the risks identified would more appropriately be described as constraints to expansion (lack of skilled staff, lack of funds) rather than risks associated with greater size (a few NGOs did mention such risks as declining quality of work or loss of focus). It would appear that NGOs were quite ambitious, but perhaps not aware of the dangers associated with expansion, in particular rapid expansion. At any rate, most NGOs (84%) reported that they planned to expand their programmes – either by adding activities to existing programmes (49 out of 56, or 88%, with expansion plans), adding new sectors or programmes (about half), or by expanding to new geographical areas (33%). Many will be expanding by pursuing two or all of these strategies.

Although this research did not specifically study the 'aid chain' between the original donor and the ultimate beneficiary, some observations can be made. The aid chain for Myanmar would look relatively short, as many of the major intermediaries (multilateral banks, major donor agencies, major consulting firms) are absent from the scene. The distance from the original donor to the ultimate beneficiary passed through relatively few steps.

NGO Staffing

While nearly all local NGOs (60) paid their staff in the form of a salary or allowance, the amounts were, as a rule, less competitive than those offered by international NGOs. Indeed, NGOs mentioned their difficulty in competing with INGOs in the recruitment and retention of staff. In addition, only a few NGOs had an international advisor. There were difficulties for some NGOs to receive permission to obtain a visa for international staff. From these facts it can be concluded that staff capacity is an issue for most NGOs in Myanmar.

When asked to identify the top three skills their staff needed to improve, NGO leaders identified communication as the top priority (see Table 8). This was mentioned by 24 NGOs (38%). Next were skills in specific technical fields (e.g., health, education, engineering), mentioned by 20 NGOs (31%). Computer (14 NGOs) and management skills (10 NGOs) were also mentioned. Interestingly, only three NGOs mentioned training skills and no NGOs mentioned skills such as project monitoring and evaluation, community participation, project planning, research, advocacy, behaviour change or media. The research was not able to triangulate these findings with the points of view of staff members themselves.

Table 8

Priority Skills that NGO Staff Need to Strengthen

Skills	Number of NGOs	Percentage
Communication	24	38%
Technical (e.g. health, education, engineering, etc)	20	31%
Computer	14	22%
Others	11	17%
Management	10	16%
English	9	14%
Accounting	6	9%
Training	3	5%
Answer unrelated to question	12	19%

NGO Governance, Management and Accountability

Fifty-five NGOs (or 86%) had boards of directors or executive committees governing the organisation. Policy-making responsibilities were assumed by the NGO president in six of the nine NGOs that did not have a board. Just over half (51%) of the NGOs with a board or executive committee used an open vote for selecting those members, and 11% used a secret vote. Put another way, 62% of NGOs had a recognisably democratic mode of board member selection. In contrast, 24% appointed board or executive committee members, and 5% used a method of self-selection.

The average number of members on an NGO board or executive committee was 16. The variance, however, was great, ranging from a minimum of 5 to a maximum of 100. Size of boards might differ because of different roles played by boards, though this issue was not explored in the survey. The most common frequency of meetings of the governing body was monthly (33%), followed by bi-annually (24%) and quarterly (22%); both small and large boards displayed these different meeting frequencies. One NGO board met every week, which implies a role going well beyond governance. Most NGOs (77%) reported that they had policies governing their agency. However, a significant number, 15 or 23%, reported having no such policies in place. Policies were prepared and approved by an assembly or conference (33%), by a board decision (33%), by the NGO's founders (10%), or by the decision of the NGO's members (8%). A minority of NGOs (13%) paid some form of compensation to members of their governing body.

Observers' perspectives on NGO governance reveal that some NGO boards were not functional while others were overly involved in the day-to-day activities of the NGO. Confusion of roles was evident in some cases, with NGO directors approving policy directions, or cases where NGO staff members served as board members.

When asked to assess their organisational performance, NGO leaders gave themselves high marks for skills such as Leadership and Management and Administration. (See Table 9. Note that two NGOs refused to answer this question). The main weakness identified (listed by 32 NGOs in the categories 'fair', 'weak', and 'very weak') was NGO Fundraising, with Mobilisation being the next weakest.

Table 9

NGO Leaders' Self-assessment of Strengths and Weaknesses

Organisational Skill	Excellent	Good	Fair	Weak	Very Weak
Leadership	17	36	6	2	1
Management/ Administration	10	37	11	4	0
Mobilisation	8	36	15	3	0
Fundraising	8	22	23	8	1
Accounting	8	38	14	2	0
Technical Skill	7	35	17	1	1

With regard to accountability, when asked how they ensured that expenditures were accountable and that aid reached the intended beneficiaries, most NGOs (73%) said accountability was assured by virtue of working directly with beneficiaries. Twenty-two per cent responded that they used regular reporting, monitoring and evaluation to ensure accountability, 13% reported that they announced income and expenditure statements after an audit and 6% said they included beneficiary representatives in their decision-making processes.

Are local NGOs independent? To whom are they accountable? Independence is an important criterion for judging local NGO performance throughout the world, although it is perceived very differently in different countries. In the Myanmar context, independence typically refers to independent management separate from the government, particularly the central government leaders. Measuring independence is no easy task even in ideal conditions. Although earlier sections presented data on registration and coordination with government, these are not necessarily indicators of independence or lack of independence. Some NGO leaders, during discussions as part of this research, stated clearly that they are independent organisations. When asked to explain further, they gave examples of their work that challenged government policy and practice in relation to poor and marginalised people.

NGO Coordination and Networking

On average, NGOs reported meeting about five times with another NGO during the last year. Thirty per cent reported having regular meetings with other NGOs; in practice this meant meeting regularly with just one other NGO. Half of the surveyed NGOs reported that coordination among NGOs was fair, versus one-third reporting it weak.[14] When asked, NGOs proposed a number of ideas for improving coordination among themselves, including joint implementation (mentioned by 36% of the NGOs surveyed), participation in sector coordination meetings (20%) and sharing information (19%). However, a relatively large percentage (19%) said they did not know how to improve coordination. In Myanmar, no local NGO network had been formally established as of 2004.

NGOs' perspectives about coordination between local NGOs and international NGOs were similar to those regarding coordination amongst themselves. Few regular meetings occurred involving significant numbers of representatives of both groups. When there was coordination, it was mostly bilateral, between one NGO and one INGO. Similar to the judgements made on NGO-NGO coordination, 48% of NGOs reported that INGO-NGO coordination was fair, and 31% reported that it was weak. A few NGOs indicated that coordination with INGOs was somewhat strong (11%). Table 10 shows the responses NGOs gave regarding what they think should be the relationship between a local and an international NGO. Seventy-two per cent of NGOs named training and capacity building, 67% saw an information sharing role, and 66% wished for INGOs to provide support in raising funds from other donors. A relatively large number of NGOs (26, or 41%) said the relationship should be funding only, although this response was a contradiction for some of the same NGOs that noted other roles and relationships. While a good proportion (59%) of NGOs were interested in networking with international NGOs, only a few (17%) were interested in working together on advocacy. In a related question, NGOs were asked how coordination between NGOs and INGOs could be improved. Answers included joint implementation (20%) and training (20%). However, the single most common response was that NGOs did not know (22%).

Table 10

Types of Relationships with INGOs Desired by NGOs

Skills	Number of NGOs	Percentage
Training, capacity building	46	72%
Information sharing	43	67%
Support in raising funds from other donors	42	66%
Networking	38	59%
Provision/sharing materials	34	53%
Funding only	26	41%
Advocacy	11	17%
Other	2	3%

NGOs were not asked to comment on their partnerships with UN agencies. However, during a survey of UN agencies, those agencies generally perceived these partnerships as healthy: five out of seven UN agencies described them as 'strong' and two described them as 'medium'. These representatives noted a number of positive developments in the NGO sector in Myanmar, which include improved NGO capacity, increased trust between partners, and improved relations between NGOs and government agencies. All seven surveyed UN agencies reported that their organisation had a mission or goal for strengthening civil society in Myanmar. The most common types of support that UN agencies provided to NGOs, reported by all seven surveyed UN agencies, were training, information, networking and advocacy. Other types of support included funding and material provision (six UN agencies), institutional development (five) and support for raising funds from other donors (four). Six of the seven surveyed UN agencies responded favourably to the idea of joining a network including NGOs, INGOs and UN agencies.

NGOs reported that their relationship with a government agency was generally good. More than two-thirds (69%) reported having a strong relationship, versus two NGOs reporting weak relationships. Twelve NGOs (19%) reported having no relationship, a finding that should be further investigated. Six NGOs chose not to answer this question. Table 11 shows NGOs' answers regarding the ways they interacted with government. Thirty-four per cent mentioned frequent meetings and 22% joint implementation. On the other hand, a significant number (18, or 28%) said they did not know.

Table 11

Relationship Between NGOs and Government Agencies

Type of Relationship	Number of NGOs	Percentage
Meeting frequently	22	34%
Don't know	18	28%
Joint implementation	14	22%
Other	4	6%
Share information	2	3%
Joint planning	1	2%

In terms of the government agencies with which NGOs interacted most frequently, nearly one-third of the NGOs mentioned the Ministry of Social Welfare, Relief and Resettlement as the government agency most closely related with their work, while 25% named the Ministry of Religion. The Health and Education ministries were mentioned several times, while the Ministry of Home Affairs (which handles the NGO registration process) was mentioned five times and the Ministry of Agriculture and Irrigation twice. A separate interview was conducted with the Ministry of Social Welfare. It revealed that the Ministry also views its relationship with NGOs as collaborative.[15]

As elsewhere in the world, coordination with the government does not mean, a priori, a lack of independence on the part of NGOs. Indeed, during survey discussions with both new generation and older NGOs, some NGO leaders vigorously defended the independence of their NGOs and explained ways they maintained independence in such a politically challenging environment. According to a number of observers in Myanmar, the NGO sector in general gives an impression of timidity, hesitating to state vocally or in writing opinions that contradict official information. However, according to NGOs themselves, this timidity should not be confused with a lack of independence from the government.[16] One possible indication of independence is NGO publication activity: just over half of the surveyed NGOs (53%) published materials. Those materials included books and booklets (32%), pamphlets (19%), newsletters (15%), magazines (13%) and journals (13%). Though the survey did not address the number and frequency of publications, observers noted that very few NGO publications were circulated widely. Although related to NGOs' financial means, these data also seem to point to a certain degree of reticence on the part of NGOs. The survey did not study the quality of the publications.

NGO Approaches

"If you see a baby drowning you jump in to save it; and if you see a second and a third, you do the same. Soon you are so busy saving drowning babies that you never look up to see that there is someone there throwing these babies in the river." (Edwards and Hulme 1992, p.13)

"Saving lives is not enough. You can save lives for generations. You need to develop capacity for change (in Myanmar)." (Interview with international NGO worker)

Finally, the survey explored what kind of approaches or strategies NGOs employed in their work. Although the NGO sectors have been described, the research delved into how NGOs perceived and implemented their work with beneficiaries. NGOs were classified on the basis of three strategies.

- 'Primary' intervention strategies typically include provision of welfare, charity, relief or humanitarian assistance;

- 'Secondary' intervention strategies, which could also be called the 'developmental approach', put emphasis on long-term behaviour change, community or group mobilisation, skills development and self-reliance;

- In 'tertiary' strategies, poor or marginalised people are seen as being deprived of power and control over their own lives. Interventions in this model focus on advocacy, human rights, rights-based programming, campaigning, empowerment, conscientisation, and sometimes the building of civil society itself.

Of course, categorisation is not so simple and precise. NGOs will often display more than one approach, but in general, tertiary type organisations would tend not to also display primary strategies. Secondary type organisations may display elements of either primary or tertiary strategies, though usually not both together. As organisations also evolve, some may change intervention strategies over time.

Studying the vision and mission statements, goals, objectives, and activities mentioned by the 64 NGOs (Annex C contains a table listing the mission statements for surveyed NGOs), it was apparent that most NGOs in Myanmar were using primary, and to a lesser degree, secondary strategies. Primary strategies were used to some extent by most NGOs in Myanmar, but they were the clear underpinning for the 35 'institutional' NGOs that were part of the survey group. These organisations were providing residential and other similar types of care to marginalised groups such as orphans, the aged, and the poor. Regarding the second category, the water/sanitation, community development and agriculture NGOs were clearly engaged in secondary-type strategies: conducting skills trainings, mobilisation for the formation of new groups, behaviour change communication, and so on. It appears that perhaps some of the more recently established NGOs were more likely to base their work on secondary strategies.

With regard to tertiary strategies, it would appear that a few NGOs have experimented with tertiary-type activities. However, such strategies were not implemented systematically, even among the NGOs that were generally perceived as more progressive. This conclusion was supported by interviews and discussions with both

NGO staff and with Myanmar-based observers. The adoption of tertiary strategies was deemed risky and therefore premature at this time. For example, use of advocacy as a strategy carried the risk of unfavourable reaction from the government. (Some interviewees mentioned their perception of the government's sensitivity to criticism as evidence for the difficulty of applying advocacy strategies in Myanmar.) However, it should be noted that INGOs and UN agencies interviewed were also not pushing forward tertiary-type strategies to any significant degree.[17] It should be noted that many other countries in Asia and other parts of the world have a shortage of tertiary-type organisations.

Endnotes

5. Note that none of these 10 NGOs is large in size and scope, nor are they among the better known NGOs.

6. The Myanmar Maternal and Child Welfare Association (MMCWA) was not considered sufficiently voluntary to be included as an NGO. It is, however, an organisation which works in the social welfare sector, with a strong presence throughout the country. See Annex D for more information on the MMCWA and on the Red Cross, the two largest officially sanctioned organisations in Myanamar working in the social welfare sector.

7. Note that the graph shows a projection of 27 NGOs formed in the period 2000–2009. The actual number of surveyed NGOs formed since 2000 is nine. As this was one-third of the decade, the projected total for the decade is 27.

8. In the decade of the 1930s, only one of our surveyed NGOs was formed.

9. Although in principle an organisation was required to wait until the government approves registration before it forms and operates, clearly a good number of NGOs did not follow this rule.

10. NGOs' experiences were similar regarding their applications for extensions: Most of the seventeen of the 29 registered NGOs that had applied for an extension reported it was not a difficult process (versus three who reported it as difficult). The average length of wait for approval of the extension was about 7 months, ranging from a minimum of just one month to a maximum of 34 months. Note that one NGO reported an astonishingly short waiting period of 7 days, for both its initial application and its extension. This

extremely short waiting period indicated that the NGO had a unique channel for registration, not following the standards, and thus was not included in the calculation of averages.

11. Formerly Kerenni State.

12. Formerly Karen State.

13. It should be noted that access by INGOs and NGOs to sensitive border areas, while still challenging, had nonetheless become easier in the late 1990s and early 2000s, before a change in government policy following a leadership shake-up in October 2004. Reports in 2005 indicated a gradual tightening of INGO and NGO access to some areas. Kayah and Kayin states were considered to be areas with major security risks.

14. Observers, however, tend to classify NGO coordination and networking in Myanmar as weak, for the most part blaming the lack of a 'culture of coordination' on the isolationist tendencies (survival tactics) of NGOs that took root during the BSPP era, when restrictions on NGO activity were at their peak. Other observers perceive the existence of a number of NGO 'factions' in Myanmar which do not necessarily wish to work together.

15. Ministry representatives gave a list of the institutions they have supported: 785 pre-primary schools, 147 orphanages, 128 youth centres, 88 primary night schools, 44 homes for the elderly, ten women/girls' homes, six schools for the disabled, and one home for victims of leprosy. The Ministry provides in-kind contributions, training, monitoring and financial support (in 2003, their financial support totalled approximately 70 million Kyat or US$76,000 USD). The Ministry has also assisted such organisations obtain legal recognition, through recommendations to the Ministry of Home Affairs. They support religious organisations as well as non-sectarian organisations.

16. Nevertheless, there exists the pervasive perception that NGOs in Myanmar were not sufficiently independent of the government. Interviews with representatives of UN agencies and other international organisations confirmed the existence of this perception.

17. UN agency representatives in particular seemed to expect NGOs to adopt more tertiary strategies, indicating, somewhat unfairly, dissatisfaction that more NGOs have not done so to date.

4 CBOs in Myanmar

Definition and Selection of CBOs for the Survey

As with NGOs, a number of broad criteria to define a community-based organisation were identified:

- non-profit;

- voluntary initiative;

- relative independence from political parties and organisations, and from the government;

- self-governing;

- self-perception as accountable in some way to their community;

- providing social benefits to the community (working for the benefit of some or all of the people in their community); and

- socially progressive.

To distinguish them from NGOs, CBOs were defined as working in a limited geographical area (one community and, possibly, adjacent communities). The methodology section (Annexure A) gives more detail on how CBO information was gathered. In sum, surveyors visited 140 villages and wards (10 each in all 14 states or divisions in

Myanmar),[18] in which 682 organisations were deemed to be CBOs (an average of nearly 5 per community).[19] Due to time constraints, it was decided to limit the number of in-depth CBO interviews to a maximum of five per village or ward. This decision resulted in a sample of 455 CBOs surveyed (surveyed communities might have had less than, more than, or exactly 5 CBOs). Graph 3 shows the different types of CBOs that were surveyed in depth. Nearly half (219, or 48%) were religious CBOs (and of these, nearly two-thirds were Buddhist).[20] Other common types of CBOs were Parent Teacher Associations (PTAs: 108, or 24%), social affairs CBOs (95, or 21%), agriculture CBOs (8, or 2%), and health/water/sanitation CBOs (7, or 2%). Other kinds of CBOs totalled 18, or 4%.

Graph 3. Types of CBO

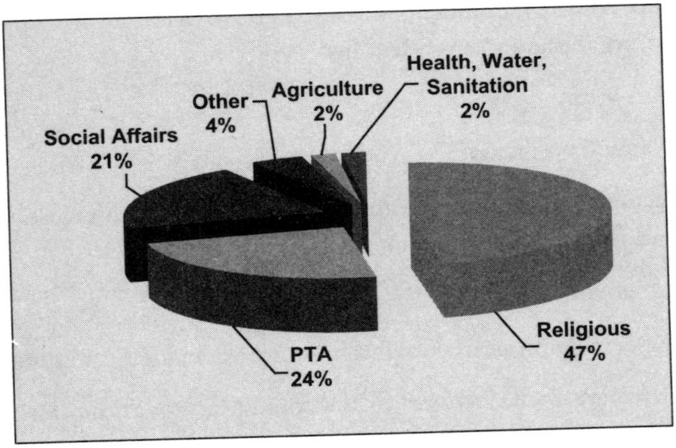

CBO Formation

Referring to Graph 4, the 1980s and 1990s were the busiest decades for new CBO formation in the survey area.[21] As noted earlier, in contrast, the 1980s was a relatively slow period for NGO formation. The 1960s and 1970s were similarly noteworthy for being relatively stagnant for NGO formation (1 and 3 surveyed NGOs respectively), but relatively vigorous for CBO formation

(55 and 44 respectively). In contrast, the 1910s, which saw the formation of six of the surveyed NGOs (a relatively high proportion), saw only one of the surveyed CBOs formed. As with NGOs, however, a very dynamic, if not explosive growth of CBOs appeared to be underway since 2000.[22]

Graph 4. Formation of New CBOs by Decade

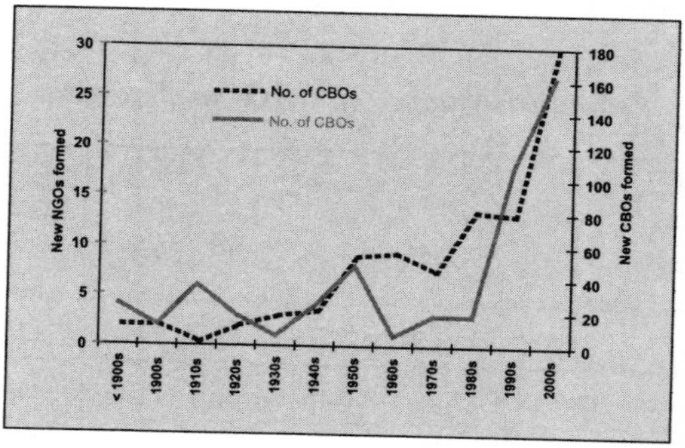

Estimated Number of CBOs in Myanmar

Based on the information collected in the survey, an attempt was made to estimate the number of CBOs in Myanmar. The survey found that there were typically more CBOs in wards than in villages. Thus, these estimates were reached by multiplying the average number of CBOs per village in each state with the total of 65,148 villages in Myanmar, and multiplying the average number of CBOs per ward with the 2,548 wards that were known to exist in 2002 (CSO 2002) – see Table 12. Using this method, it is estimated that 214,000 CBOs existed in Myanmar in 2003, representing 4,115 per 1 million population, according to the latest government population data (CSO 2002).

It should be recalled that the average of CBOs per village and ward was based on research in 114 villages and 26 wards, in 14 townships (that is, one township per state or division – please see Annexure A for more information on the research methodology). The survey deliberately did not select townships with security or access issues. It is a reasonable assumption that insecure or remote areas might have fewer CBOs. However, some research has indicated a high level of group formation on the Thai border. (South 2005) The number of CBOs may be overestimated due to the over-representation of urban wards in the survey (see Annexure A for an explanation of this over-representation).

Table 12

Estimated Number of CBOs in Myanmar

	State/ Division	Villages in Survey	CBOs in Rural Areas	Estimated Total	Wards in Survey	CBOs in Urban Areas	Estimated Total CBOs	Estimated Total
1	Shan	15,513	2.6	40,722	336	3.5	1,176	41,898
2	Ayeyarwady	11,651	2.7	31,458	219	7.8	1,715	33,172
3	Magway	4,774	5.3	25,302	160	7.8	1,253	26,555
4	Mandalay	5,472	3.0	16,416	259	5.0	1,295	17,711
5	Chin	1,355	10.4	14,058	29	12.5	363	14,421
6	Bago	6,498	2.0	12,996	246	2.0	492	13,488
7	Rakhine	3,871	2.7	10,452	120	7.8	940	11,391
8	Kayin	2,092	4.3	9,058	46	12.0	552	9,610
9	Sagaing	6,095	1.3	8,125	171	7.8	1,339	9,464
10	Kachin	2,630	2.7	7,101	116	4.0	464	7,565
11	Mon	1,199	4.6	5,461	69	17.0	1,173	6,634
12	Yangon	2,119	3.8	8,152	685	8.3	5,686	13,837
13	Tanintharyi	1,255	4.1	5,199	63	6.0	378	5,577
14	Kayah	624	4.2	2,652	29	8.0	232	2,884
	Total	65,148		197,152	2,548		17,056	214,208

A reorganisation of Table 12 more clearly compares the relative concentration of CBOs in villages and wards in each of Myanmar's 7 States and 7 Divisions. In Table 13, it can be seen that four states (Chin, with an astonishing 10 CBOs per village, Mon, Kayin and Kayah) were in the top five (villages in Magway Division also had high CBO density).

Table 13

Average Number of CBOs Per Village (Rural)
and Ward (Urban)

State/Division	CBOs Per Village (Rural)	CBOs Per Ward (Urban)
Chin (S)	10.4	12.5
Magway (D)	5.3	7.8
Mon (S)	4.6	17.0
Kayin (S)	4.3	12.0
Kayah (S)	4.2	8.0
Taninthayi (D)	4.1	6.0
Yangon (D)	3.8	8.3
Mandalay (D)	3.0	5.0
Rakhine (S)	2.7	7.8
Kachin (S)	2.7	4.0
Shan (S)	2.6	3.5
Ayeyarwady (D)	2.7	7.8
Bago (D)	2.0	2.0
Sagaing (D)	1.3	7.8

In similar fashion, surveyed urban wards in states, rather than divisions, tended to have higher degrees of CBO density – Mon State, with an average 17 CBOs per ward, followed by Chin (12.5) and Kayin (12). However, what is more noteworthy still is the higher density of CBOs in urban wards compared to villages overall: fully 10 states and divisions display higher CBO density in urban wards (6 or higher) than the second-placed Magway Division's density of 5.3 CBOs per village. This would appear to be a very interesting field for further study.

CBO Sectors and Beneficiaries

When asked in what priority sectors they worked, by far the greatest number of CBOs (236, or 52%) reported working in the religious sector (and 36, or 8% reported working in construction of religious buildings). Notably, this exceeded the number of CBOs who identified themselves as religious CBOs (219). As with the results of the self-identification exercise, CBOs were then most active in social welfare and education (30% and 26% respectively). Another 5% mentioned school construction (see Table 14).

CBOs were asked to name their primary group of beneficiaries. Annexure E shows a table listing the detailed answers that CBOs gave to this question. Table 15 attempts to further categorise these responses. The survey found that CBOs defined their beneficiaries either broadly, or inclusively, (i.e., any member of the community, or specific groups within the community but not based on CBO membership, or on membership in a particular ethnic or religious group), or in terms of specific affiliations (i.e., beneficiaries were limited to members of a particular group, usually CBO members, or of a particular religious group).

Table 14

CBO Priority Sectors

Sector	Number of CBOs	Percentage
Religious	236	52%
Social Welfare	135	30%
Education	118	26%
Construction of Religious Buildings	36	8%
School Construction	21	5%
Community Development	13	3%
Agriculture and Livestock	11	2%
Preservation of Traditions and Culture	8	2%
Health	7	2%
Water	2	<1%
Construction (general)	1	<1%
Human Trafficking	1	<1%
Sanitation	1	<1%

Note: CBOs were allowed to name more than one intervention sector.

From the table, it can be seen that 59% of CBOs considered themselves as benefiting the wider community (in general terms, for example, 'people in the community', or in a focused way, for example, 'children from poor families'). This figure was quite striking given that CBOs tend to be member-based, self-help organisations whose benefits tend generally to accrue to the members themselves (unlike NGOs whose beneficiaries, by definition, must not include anyone closely associated with the organisation itself, such as staff or board members). This group also included the significant number of religious CBOs who defined their beneficiaries broadly (72, or 32% of 219 Religious CBOs). In addition to this, 59% were those CBOs who offered their help to people outside their main beneficiary group (2% of membership-based groups and 5% of groups primarily helping co-religionists also extended their services to others beyond the group). The table also shows that all PTA groups extended their benefits generally, as did all Health and Wat/San CBOs.

Table 15

CBO Beneficiaries

Type of Beneficiaries, Defined:	Religious Affairs	Social Affairs	PTA	Health, Wat/San	Agric.	Other	Total	
Broadly, community	72	69	108	7		12	268	59%
Solely denominationally	101	3				1	105	23%
Primarily denominationally, but includes other groups	22	2					24	5%
Solely membership based	22	12			8	2	44	10%
Primarily membership-based, but includes others	2	9					11	2%
Other						3	3	<1%
Total	219	95	108	7	8	18	455	

Note: CBOs were only allowed to name one category of beneficiary, though a number of these categories contain multiple sub-categories. See Annexure E for more details about the definitions used in this table.

In contrast, twenty-three per cent of CBOs stipulated that beneficiaries had to have the same religious affiliation as the CBO itself. It is reasonable to assume that the 22 Religious CBOs which characterised their beneficiaries according to membership could just have likely been included in the 'solely denomination' category (bringing that total to 123 from 101 – this would bring the total of CBOs strictly serving members of the same religion to 28%). Finally, for another 10% of CBOs, beneficiaries had to be members of the CBO (of which, all Agriculture CBOs surveyed extended support strictly to their members).

To complete the analysis of CBOs' beneficiary reach, an additional survey was conducted. This survey attempted to reach the poorest of the poor, and in particular to find out their perceptions on CBOs in their villages. This survey reached 188 households representing the poorest members of their communities.[23] (Annexure A contains a more detailed description of the methodology.) The results of this survey were surprising, particularly when compared to the information given by CBOs on their beneficiaries, as presented earlier. Out of the 188 households, only 19 (or 10%) reported having received assistance from a CBO in the past 12 months. It should be noted that this survey was conducted in entirely different villages than those surveyed in the CBO survey, which therefore presents the (remote) possibility that these 188 villages had much lower levels of CBO density than found in the CBO survey. However, there is nothing particular about the 188 villages selected (for example, much higher insecurity) that would suggest, a priori, that CBO density should be lower. Of the organisations that were mentioned, most of these were not even CBOs as defined in this research. Rather, organisations like the Myanmar Maternal and Child Welfare Association and the Village Peace and Development Council (mentioned five times each) were the most frequently cited.[24]

Clearly, further research on whether and why poorest households seemed to be excluded by civil society social welfare organisations would be very useful indeed. One possibility raised by the findings has to do with employment – the survey found that 67% of main income earners in the household were engaged in daily labour, while 10% had farming as their main occupation. This could indicate that members of the poorest households were particularly mobile, which, along with the obvious economic instability they must endure, might also explain why CBOs and other organisations would find it difficult to reach them. Though a number of other plausible causes may exist that would explain why poorest households reported such low levels of assistance by CBOs,[25] it would appear likely that one of the main reasons was that CBOs, and indeed other organisations, did not make a particular effort to direct their assistance to the poorest of the poor. The survey found that only 107 (57%) of poorest households were even able to name a single social welfare organisation in their village.

CBO Funding

CBOs have been generating substantial volumes of funds. On average, each of the 360 CBOs that responded to a question requesting budget information received an average of 288,000 Kyats (or $314) only from resources inside the community. Each CBO received on average an additional 190,000 (or $207) from other sources of funding outside the community or other sources. The combined total average annual income of each CBO, therefore, was approximately $521.

Further analysis was used to try to determine the average funding level for rural-based CBOs, leading to very surprising results. Among the 360 CBOs that provided budget information, 271 were based in rural villages. The average amount of funds they generated just within their communities during the past year was equivalent to US$438 per CBO. This means that each rural CBO was collecting significantly more funds than each urban CBO, on average. The urban areas where wealth was concentrated and where population density was much greater, would logically be expected to donate more from each household to CBOs or, at the very least, more funds overall, given the much larger number of households per CBO. However, the rural villages were far ahead in terms of giving. As almost every rural village had at least 1 CBO, and many (depending on the number of households) had 5 or more, this would mean that CBOs were generating very large amounts of funds from each household.

Further analysis allowed an estimation of household contributions to CBOs. The total number of households in the rural villages was approximately 17,000. The amount of funding generated in the rural villages in the survey was approximately 60 million Kyat, or the equivalent of approximately US $65,000. On average, each household contributed approximately 3,500 Kyat to CBOs last year, or approximately US$3.8. The research did not break down the amounts in terms of allocations to religious institutions (temples, churches, mosques) and non-sectarian groups. In the urban wards, using the same method for calculation, each household contributed an average of $1.6 to CBOs.

This would indicate that rural people, the majority of whom were earning less than the equivalent of $150 annually, were contributing over 2% of their income to CBOs. Might this significant redistribution of wealth at the local level help explain why some of the indicators of poverty were so low in such a low-income country?[26] Or was most of this money going into building religious structures, not giving any direct or indirect material benefit to the poor and marginalised? Further in-depth poverty studies looking at many factors, including the distribution of wealth, would be required to understand what exactly has been happening in the rural villages around Myanmar.

Maybe for the people of Myanmar and those familiar with Myanmar this would not seem so surprising. In the rural areas, many of the methods for collecting funds were based on social cohesion. While a villager who decided not to pay an amount to a CBO would not face imprisonment, that person or household would likely face some degree of social isolation. The social pressure on each rural household to donate a 'fair share' was probably very high in the villages. The social pressure on urban households, however, was probably not very intense. In the Myanmar language and in Myanmar tradition, these were described as voluntary contributions. People in Western countries might describe these as non-voluntary contributions because of the high degree of social pressure. This survey was unable to study in depth the degree of pressure placed on households to make donations.

Community fundraising would be an interesting study for future researchers, especially as many of the schools, roads and other village-level infrastructure were constructed in this way. The CBO survey studied the presence of government health clinics and schools and asked the villagers who initiated these. The survey found that most of the surveyed villages/wards (76%) had schools, and in most cases (46%) community elders initiated them. It is likely the community financed all or most of the school. The Ministry of Education has stated on many occasions that the people in Myanmar valued education and supported school construction in the country, implying that the government did not finance school construction, passing the responsibility to communities. The Ministry of Education budget has not included sufficient funding for school construction. The survey also found that the local leader (chairman of VPDC) initiated 37% of the schools, villagers in general 21%, Buddhist monks 6% and teachers 5%. Only 24% of the communities had a health clinic. Community elders again initiated most (15) of the 34 clinics, followed by VPDC chairman (13), the Health Department (12) and villagers in general (2).

Studying the various types of CBO fund raising, the research found another type of local pressure. Two common methods, given by 13% and 11% of CBOs, respectively, comprised the collection of funds through a sort of household assessment either using a flat rate or a variable rate depending on wealth. This may indicate a high degree of social pressure. Membership fees (16%) may represent a similar type of pressure. Such fees were common among many but not all PTAs. Sometimes monthly fees were collected for each student, but the amounts were apparently small, approximately 25 Kyats (US$0.03) per student in some areas. However, voluntary methods of collecting funds were also common: voluntary collections from households (33%) and opening a collection box (11%).

Overall, most CBOs (360, or 79%) collected funds in their communities, while nearly one-third of the CBOs (32%) received funds from outside their communities. It is interesting to note that some CBOs reported no fundraising either from within or from outside their community. For example, seven of the eight agriculture CBOs received no funding at all. The 360 CBOs that responded to questions requesting budget information collected an average of US$314 per CBO in 2002 from sources inside the community, and an additional US$207 from sources outside the community, giving a total average annual income of US$521 per CBO.

Most CBOs indicated that the level of difficulty in fund raising had remained about the same as in previous years (37%), while a large number reported that it was becoming easier (28%). Only 19% said it was becoming more difficult. PTAs seemed to experience the most difficulty while religious CBOs seemed to find it easier. Comparing member and non-member CBOs,[27] the most significant difference was the higher ratio of member CBOs who reported not needing funds. Overall, this would indicate that there was no crisis in fund raising, despite the economic conditions in the country and the reliance of CBOs on local community donations.

CBO Governance, Management and Accountability

Most CBOs (72%) used an open vote for choosing committee members. Only 4% used a secret ballot. Some CBOs (15%) chose committee members by appointing them, and 7% of the CBOs allowed members to select themselves, possibly seeking volunteers. Committee members' meeting frequency varied from three to four times per year for PTAs, five times per year for religious CBOs and six times per year for social affairs CBOs.

CBOs were asked to name the qualifications for being eligible to stand for CBO committee membership. As it was an open question, a great number of qualifications were expressed (and CBOs were allowed to name more than one quality). Suffice to say that by far the most cited qualification (by 285 or 63%) was the ability to give time to the CBO. Next in importance was leadership or skill (130 CBOs, or 29%). Interestingly, the next most cited qualifications (respectively by 27%, 23% and 23%) were all ethical or moral qualifications (trustworthiness, piety, and good morals, respectively). Educational qualifications were only cited by 48 CBOs, or 11%.

CBO governance was far from gender- or age-balanced. CBOs had an average of 7.1 male committee members compared with 1.6 female members. The gender balance improved a little among non-sectarian CBOs (2:7) compared with religious CBOs (1:8). About half of CBOs (49%) had no female committee members at all (contrasting with 9% with no male members). Fourteen CBOs (3%) included one or more children serving on the committee. Nearly all CBOs (95%) did not pay committee members any form of compensation. Among the 25 CBOs who did pay compensation, the most common form of payment was donation (nine CBOs), while three paid a salary.

When asked to identify the top three skills that CBO staff, members or volunteers needed to improve, the most important skills were organising skills (mentioned by 167, or 37%, of the CBOs) and leadership/management skills (142 CBOs, or 31%). The next most common responses were religious skills (81, or 18%), fundraising skills (56, or 12%) and accounting skills (50, or 11%). Forty-four CBOs (10%) mentioned no skills improvement being necessary because CBO tasks did not require any technical skills.

The survey's question on accountability seems not to have been understood by all respondents: when asked how CBOs accounted for the use of funds given to them by the community and/or outside sources, 14% of CBOs stated that the funds were used for religious buildings. However, 40% did reply that assistance was given upon revision and approval of accounts and balance sheets by authorised persons or relevant organisations (another 15% replied that assistance was given with the approval of authorised persons or relevant organisations). When asked about whether and how CBOs ensured fair distribution of benefits, most of the CBOs (55%) said fairness was ensured by following decisions made by authorised persons or from meetings.

CBO Coordination and Networking

A surprisingly high number of CBOs (304, or 67%) said they did not coordinate with a government agency during the last year. Among the 151 who did coordinate, most coordination occurred at township level. Half of the 151 CBOs coordinated with the Township Education Department (it can be assumed that these were all PTAs; indeed, Table 16 shows that a PTA majority of 69% coordinated with the government, 29% coordinated with the Township Peace and Development Council, 17% with the Township Health Centre, and 10% with the Township Religious Affairs Department. Only three CBOs mentioned dealing with State/Division level representatives, and only two at national level.

When studying the specific responses, it would appear that many of the 151 CBOs were not working in 'partnership' with the government, but rather simply seeking permission. The PTAs appeared to be a significant exception, as they were an intrinsic part of the formal education system in Myanmar. The method for coordination included requesting permission directly or through contact persons for the relevant activity. Thirteen CBOs reported receiving an inspection and suggestions from the government agency from whom they sought assistance.

Table 16

CBO Coordination with Government in the Past Year

Type of Organisation	Coordinated	Did not Coordinate	Total
PTA	75	33	108
Religious	52	167	219
Social Affairs	13	82	95
Agriculture	4	4	8
Other	4	14	18
Health, Water and Sanitation	3	4	7
Total	**151**	**304**	**455**

In contrast, the majority of CBOs (386, or 85%) reported having some communication and coordination with other organisations in their villages or wards during the last year (Table 17). By far, the most common local organisation contacted was the Village (or Ward) Peace and Development Council. Though a branch of the government administration reaching every community in the country, surveyed CBOs classified them not as government agencies but as 'other' organisations. Most common reasons given for seeking out other organisations included seeking assistance for holding religious festivals, repairing school buildings, and providing assistance at funerals.

A large percentage of CBOs went outside their village to communicate or coordinate with organisations from neighbouring villages or wards (41% in the last year). Most CBOs (85%) would have liked to work more closely with other CBOs or NGOs. More than half (54%) said the reason was to obtain funding and assistance, for 10% it was for the purpose of developing the CBO or village, while another 8% mentioned for training and technical assistance. Finally, few (47, or 10%) CBOs reported having connections with international organisations; religious and agriculture CBOs tended to be least connected in this regard. PTAs had connection with UNICEF in the education sector, and a good number of health-related CBOs (including water and sanitation organisations) were formed with the assistance of international NGOs or UN agencies. Among the 47 CBOs with connections with international organisations, UNICEF and UNDP were mentioned the most (63%).

Table 17

CBO Coordination or Communication with Other Local Organisations

Type of Organisation	Linked	Not Linked	Total
Religious	188	31	219
PTA	95	13	108
Social Affairs	83	12	95
Other	11	7	18
Health, Water and Sanitation	6	1	7
Agriculture	3	5	8
Total	386	69	455

CBO Future Roles

The NGOs were asked their opinion on the role of CBOs. A majority (55%) responded that CBOs had a participation and cooperation role. Fourteen per cent did not know what their role should be. Other responses included providing leadership and management (8%), helping the community (8%), providing technical assistance and knowledge (5%) and mobilising people

(3%). When the CBOs were asked this question, 52% said they should cooperate in relevant sectors, 40% said they should lead or guide in the relevant sectors, while 21% said they should organise. It would appear that this question was not well understood by a good number of CBOs.

The seven surveyed UN agencies described the main role of CBOs differently from the main role of NGOs. They generally saw CBOs as more directly involved in working with beneficiaries, as would be expected. Three of the UN agencies mentioned direct implementation and another three mentioned community mobilisation, participation and empowerment as main roles for CBOs. However, two UN agencies saw CBOs as having an important role in advocacy, while another saw a role in local governance.

Endnotes

18. Surveyors visited 140 communities (26 urban wards and 114 rural villages) in 14 of Myanmar's 324 townships. Note that there are 65,148 villages and 2,548 wards in Myanmar according to 2001 figures. As explained further in the methodology section, the survey was biased against relatively insecure and remote villages, and gives urban wards greater weight (1 per 4 villages surveyed) than was warranted based on their proportion in Myanmar (1 per 25 villages nationally).

19. An additional 602 organisations were found in the same 140 villages, but these were not deemed to meet the study's definition of a CBO. They included: Village (Ward) Peace and Development Councils (140), Union Solidarity and Development Association (92), Myanmar Maternal and Child Welfare Association (87), Auxiliary Fire Brigade (76), School Trustees Association (60), Women's Affairs Committee (58), People's militia, Village Defence Association, People's Power (50), Red Cross (27), Veteran's Association (9), and Cooperatives (3).

20. Sixty-four per cent were Buddhist, 23 % Christian, 10% Muslim and 3.2% Hindu.

21. As with NGO growth, the graph shows a projection of 177 CBOs formed in the period 2000–2009. The actual number of surveyed

CBOs formed since 2000 is 59, bringing the total formed since 1990 to 152, or 33% of surveyed CBOs. Note that 15 CBOs did not know their date of formation.

22. As noted in the NGO section earlier, this survey does not capture CBOs formed in any of these periods that no longer exist.

23. The average daily expenditure among the 188 poorest households was approximately US$1.1, with average household size of five members.

24. Saving and Credit Organisation, established by UNDP as part of their Human Development Initiative project, was mentioned four times, INGOs three times. Other groups mentioned were Buddhist groups (2), Christian churches (2), a social affairs group (1) and a school committee (1). Surprisingly, no respondents mentioned receiving any assistance from Myanmar Red Cross Society, nor from local NGOs.

25. Other possible reasons include: 1) the fact that so many CBOs were engaged in activities whose benefits were not directed to specific households but to the community at large, such as religious works, or education, indeed the two most common kinds of CBOs identified in our survey. In the case of the latter, poor households might not cite, say, school construction as a benefit to themselves either because it was not directed specifically to them or because they might not send their children to school at all; 2) the possibility that interviewees provided inaccurate information, either because they were nervous about their participation in the survey, or perhaps because they hoped to eventually gain from underreporting benefits received from CBOs.

26. Myanmar is an economic paradox. The people have some of the lowest incomes in the world. (EIU 2002 p.18)) In 2001, the average household expenditure on food rose to 71%, comparing poorly with a global estimate of 50% as an indicator of poverty. (UNICEF 2001 pp.36–37) The rate of malnutrition, in terms of moderately or severely under weight children, is 35.3%. (UNICEF 2001 p.62) Yet , the portion of the population living in absolute poverty, below the official poverty line, is lower in Myanmar (22.9%) than in many other countries in the region, and, unlike patterns in other countries, poverty is evenly spread between rural and urban areas. (ADB 2001 pp.12–13)

27. Of the 455 CBOs surveyed, 150 were member-based, and 305 non-member based.

5 Conclusions

Civil society is alive in Myanmar today. In fact, it never died. Clearly, NGOs and CBOs survived throughout recent history. NGOs and CBOs that formed decades or a century past, still exist and function today. New NGOs and CBOs were continuously forming every decade. In fact, the country may be on the verge of an explosion of new organisations. More NGOs and CBOs were forming since 1990 than at any other time in history. The 1950s and the current era (1988–present) were periods of relatively brisk formation of new NGOs (relative to the BSPP era and the period of British colonial rule). Extrapolating from the number of surveyed NGOs, it is estimated that Myanmar may have had approximately 270 NGOs operating in the country in 2003, which would appear to be a respectable figure compared with other countries in general, including other countries in the region. In addition, it is estimated that Myanmar may have had up to 214,000 CBOs in 2003. Even if this number is somewhat overestimated, it appears that there is extensive CBO coverage throughout the country.

Just over half of the NGOs surveyed were registered or in the process of registering with the government. Two-thirds of the registered NGOs felt that the process of registering was not overly difficult. The length of time to register averaged 8 months. Nearly all of the registered NGOs were registered under the Organisation of Association Law (1988).

Between them, the NGOs surveyed operated programmes in all 14 states and divisions. NGO operations were reasonably evenly split between the 7 states and 7 divisions. Tanintharyi and Magway Divisions, and Rakhine and Kayah States, were least-served by the Yangon-based NGOs.

Sectors in which at least 20% of surveyed NGOs worked were: health (25 NGOs), religious affairs (22), social welfare (21), water and sanitation (15), HIV/AIDS (14) and agriculture (12). NGOs reported that most of their programming funds went to health (19%), social welfare (12%), agriculture (11%) and education (7%). Very little funding was spent on: water and sanitation (3%), HIV/AIDS (2%), nutrition (<1%), conflict resolution (<1%), emergency response (<1%) and human rights (<1%).

The average annual budget of the NGOs surveyed was US\$38,300, but ranged from US\$440 to US\$500,000. The single largest source of funds for the NGOs surveyed was from INGOs (40%), while the next largest contributors (comprising about one-third of NGO budgets) came from public donations. There was some confusion about the relative importance of UN contributions to the NGOs surveyed. NGOs reported that UN contributions amounted to <1% of their annual budgets. However, UN agencies' figures contradicted the NGOs' reported figures.

Over half of the NGOs surveyed had formal and recognisably democratic procedures for selecting board members. Only a few of the NGOs surveyed felt that coordination and networking amongst NGOs was good. In terms of the government agencies with which NGOs interacted most frequently, nearly one-third of the NGOs mentioned the Ministry of Social Welfare, Relief and Resettlement as the government agency most closely related with their work, while 25% named the Ministry of Religion. More than two-thirds of NGOs reported having a strong relationship with the government; NGO interviews revealed many NGOs' commitment to maintain independence from the government.

NGOs in Myanmar seemed to be implementing primarily social welfare and charity-type of programmes ('primary' strategy), though a significant number were increasingly engaging in activities that could be characterised as forming a 'secondary' approach. Very few NGOs in Myanmar were engaged in advocacy and other activities that make up a 'tertiary' or rights-based approach. One of the biggest challenges facing Myanmar NGOs was human resource development – typically, the best staff members tend to be recruited by INGOs and UN agencies.

The research found that just over half of all CBOs surveyed worked primarily on issues related to religion, but many also worked on social welfare (30%) and education (26%). Over half of the CBOs surveyed claimed to work for the benefit of the 'wider community', not just their own members.

Three-quarters of the CBOs surveyed collected funds in their community during the last year and nearly one-third received funds from outside their community. The total collected by CBOs was US$237,055, with an average annual CBO budget of US$521. Only one-fifth of the CBOs surveyed said fundraising was becoming more difficult, but PTAs were more likely than other CBOs to find fundraising difficult.

Nearly three-quarters of the CBOs surveyed used open votes to choose their committee members. CBO committee membership was clearly dominated by men, with nearly half of the CBOs surveyed having no female committee members. Only 3% of the CBOs surveyed had any children on their committees.

Two-thirds of the CBOs surveyed said that they did not coordinate with any government agency, even though most PTAs did so. Three-quarters of the CBOs surveyed said that they communicated or coordinated with the Village (or Ward) Peace and Development Council in their community. A high percentage (41%) of CBOs communicate or coordinate with organisations from neighbouring villages or wards. Only 10% of the CBOs surveyed reported having connections with international organisations; these were primarily PTAs with links to UNICEF and some other CBOs who mentioned a relationship with UNDP.

Looking at the issue of value and quality, civil society organisations in Myanmar have made a great deal of progress. They have shown a great deal of motivation in forming their organisations, managing difficult situations and implementing a wide range of interventions, sometimes aimed at alleviating poverty and helping marginalised people. They have tried some innovative and bold approaches. They have avoided some of the pitfalls that typically befall local NGOs. NGOs in Myanmar have some advantages over their cousins in many other Asian countries. They have not been rocked by financial scandals. They have not united together in networks only to later split apart. They have not taken their squabbles into the public realm. They have not pandered to fundamentalism. They have not faced an anti-NGO lobby. They have not lost touch with the grassroots in an effort to become ever more sophisticated. They have not evolved into an elite and segregated group. They have not frequently tripped over each other's toes in the competition to claim certain beneficiaries or geographical areas as their own. They have not sprung up a host of artificial NGOs.

However, before they become complacent, they should remember that they have many more weaknesses in other areas than their cousins. They have not launched any successful national campaigns leading to significant policy changes. They have not fought vigorously for protecting the rights of suffering people, whether the suffering was caused by government action or inaction or exploitation by businesses or other causes. They have not struggled and grown through their unity against oppression. Their programming strategies have not evolved, but rather stayed at mostly a primary level focusing on direct welfare and service provision. That situation continues today for the majority of NGOs and the vast majority of CBOs. NGOs and CBOs are neglecting poverty issues. They have not regained very much of the lost dynamism and lost ground from the past 40 years. They have not developed deep roots in the soils of social justice. They have not successfully protected the environment on a large scale. They have not done numerous things that their cousins have done.

Accountability and independence were under challenge. There is still an assumption that local NGOs in Myanmar might be tainted by association with the military government. NGOs in general have not effectively countered that perception. Human resources and governance were weakened during the years of repression, and NGOs are still trying to catch up and develop their human resource capacities. Fund raising followed traditional patterns. Coordination and networking remain poor, following the decades of isolation.

Finally, based on the experience of NGOs around the world, and based on the results of this research, the following recommendations are proposed as being most relevant to NGOs and CBOs at this juncture in the development of Myanmar civil society. NGOs should open the dialogue on core social issues, particularly poverty and marginalisation, perhaps through conferences or other events. They could gradually raise the public's awareness on the causes of poverty, together with international partners. Together they could also gradually raise awareness with the Myanmar government about the role of civil society.

While adopting a sudden and radical approach with advocacy in Myanmar would likely be harmful to individual NGOs and possibly civil society as a whole, a more gradual and subtle strategy used in many countries where governments do not tolerate NGOs that challenge official policy openly is to wrap the programme up in layers. On the outside, the NGO intervention appears to be simple and non-threatening. It appears to be a simple social welfare programme. It appears to be a simple community development programme. However, the NGO intentionally builds many layers around the intervention so that inside, there is a 'complex empowerment strategy'. (Fowler 1997 p.121) While some INGOs in Myanmar understand and may try to practise this layering, the local NGOs are generally not familiar nor practising this. INGOs and UN agencies can help them develop this approach.

NGOs should pay more attention to the issue of independence. Their credibility in Myanmar and throughout the world rests on this. Although there are no definitive criteria to be applied, these can be developed. Some criteria could include frequency of meetings between an NGO's senior staff and high-ranking government leaders, inclusion of these government leaders in NGO publications, the internal process for making decisions about programming location, the level and type of participatory management, the level of consultation and rigorous research for making programming decisions, the level and credibility of analysis of the situation of people in the specified geographic area, and the consistency of messages from the NGO when it talks with the government and when it talks with others.

NGOs, INGOs, UN agencies and other civil society participants should increase the contacts among themselves to increase mutual understanding. One specific important initiative would be establishing meaningful coordination bodies for specific thematic or sector issues. INGOs and UN agencies would be in an ideal position to take this initiative. They would need to build trust and create a space for local NGOs. They should also explore further some opportunities to increase information sharing, networking and joint projects.

Capacity of NGOs (skills, knowledge and experience of staff) is a very critical area to address in the short term and long term. INGOs and the UN agencies should support capacity building through funding and training efforts to strengthen programmatic, administrative and managerial capacity. NGOs should give capacity building within their organisations a higher priority. In addition, INGOs and the UN should examine the impact of their hiring processes on the ability of NGOs to attract and retain qualified personnel.

One other very critical human resource factor is leadership. While it will be important to consider and embark on some or many of the possible ways to progress civil society, it will first of all require leadership. In the conclusion of a book detailing the growth of some of the most renowned South Asian civil society organisations known globally for innovative and progressive work, one of the key factors cited was leadership. Bold individuals came forward and sparked impressive movements joined by large numbers of impatient and ambitious people who wanted change in their societies. (Smillie and Hailey 2001 p.173)

INGOs, the UN and donors should strive to simplify their funding arrangements with NGOs, and offer support to NGOs to navigate donor requirements. Some donors should consider a grant fund that small local NGOs could apply for in Myanmar language. Also, a grant fund of very small amounts (under US$10,000) would be very useful for a large number of small NGOs.

Finally, this research points to a number of areas where future research could provide valuable insight. A major topic of inquiry should include poverty in Myanmar. In addition to studying the dimensions of poverty and how it is experienced in the different parts of the country, an in-depth look at how civil society organisations interact with the poorest of the poor would be valuable. Another important topic for further study is civil society and gender. Gender was not specifically analysed in this research. A very interesting future study could revolve around the gender dimension in Myanmar's evolving civil society. Other interesting topics for study would include the role of religion in forming

NGOs and CBOs, and the reasons for the varying proportions of NGOs and CBOs within each religious group.

Further study on fund raising and sources of funding for NGOs and CBOs would bring greater understanding to this area. Included in this could be a study on the degree to which people are free to choose the CBOs to support financially (and how much to contribute). The contrast between population density and level of giving suggests another interesting area for future study.

6 Bibliography

Asian Development Bank (1999) *A Study of NGOs*, Manila, The Philippines

– (2001) *Country Economic Report Myanmar*, Manila, The Philippines

Bennett, Jon (1995) Meeting Needs, *NGO Coordination in Practice*, Earthscan, London

Cady, John F (1958) *A History of Modern Burma*, Cornell University Press, Ithaca, NY, US

Central Statistical Organisation, Government of the Union of Myanmar (2001) *Statistical Yearbook*, Yangon, Myanmar

Chambers, Robert (1992) 'Spreading And Self-Improving: A Strategy for Scaling-up' in Edwards, Michael and Hulme, David *Making a Difference: NGOs and Development in a Changing World*, Earthscan, London, pp.40–48

Department of Health Planning, Government of the Union of Myanmar, and UNICEF (2000) *Multiple Indicator Cluster Survey*, Yangon, Myanmar

Department of Labour, Government of the Union of Myanmar, and UNFPA (2002) *Handbook on Human Resources Development Indicators*, Yangon, Myanmar

Economist Intelligence Unit (2002) *Country Profile 2002 Myanmar (Burma)*, London

Edwards, Michael and Hulme, David (2002) 'NGO Performance and Accountability: Introduction and Overview', in Edwards, Michael and Fowler, Alan *NGO Management*, Earthscan, London

Fernando, Udan (2003) *NGOs in Sri Lanka Past and Present Trends*, Wasala Publications, Nugegoda, Sri Lanka

Fisher, Julie (1997), *Non-Governments, NGOs and the Political Development of the Third World*, Kumarian Press, Bloomfield, US

Fowler, Alan (1997) *Striking A Balance, A Guide to Enhancing the Effectiveness of Non-Governmental Organisastions in International Development*, Earthscan, London

Furnivall, J S (1960) *The Governance of Modern Burma*, Institute of Pacific Relations, NY US

Horton, Scott and Kazakina, Alla (1999) 'The Legal Regulation of NGOs: Central Asia at a Crossroads', in Ruffin, M Holt and Waugh, Daniel C *Civil Society in Central Asia*, University of Washington Press, Seattle, US, pp.34–55

Howell, Jude and Pearce, Jenny (2001) *Civil Society & Development: A Critical Exploration*, Lynne Rienner Publishers, London

Hudson, Mike (2002) *Managing Without Profit*, Directory of Social Change, London

ICG-International Crisis Group (2002) *Myanmar: The Politics of Humanitarian Aid*, Brussels

ILO-International Labour Office (2001), 282nd Session, 'Developments concerning the question of the observance by the Government of Myanmar of the Forced Labour Convention, 1930 (No. 29)' Geneva

Korten, David C, (1990) *Getting to the 21st Century: Voluntary Action and the Global Agenda*, Kumarian Press, West Hartford US

Kothari, Smitu (1999) "Inclusive, Just, Plural, Dynamic: Building a 'Civil' Society in the Third World," in Eade, Deborah (ed) *Development and Social Action* Development in Practice Readers, Oxfam, Oxford

Lewis, David (2001) *The Management of Non-Governmental Development Organisations*, Routledge, London

Liddell, Zunetta (1999) 'No Room to Move: Legal Constraints on Civil Society in Burma', in *Strengthening Civil Society in Burma, Possibilities and Dilemmas for International NGOs*, Burma Center Netherlands and Transnational Institute, Silkworm Books, Chiang Mai, Thailand, pp.54–68

Ministry of Information, Government of the Union of Myanmar (2002) *Myanmar Facts and Figures 2002*, Yangon, Myanmar

Nash, Manning (1965) *The Golden Road to Modernity: Village Life in Contemporary Burma*, John Wiley & Sons, Inc., New York, US

Pearce, Jenny (2000) 'Development, NGOs, and Civil Society: The Debate and Its Future', in Eade, Deborah (ed) *Development, NGOs, and Civil Society* Development in Practice Readers, Oxfam, Oxford, pp.15–43

Pinheiro, Paulo Sergio (2003) Statement to the 59th Session of the Commission on Human Rights, Item 9, Geneva

Purcell, Marc (1999) '"Axe-handles or Willing Minions?:' International NGOs in Burma," in *Strengthening Civil Society in Burma, Possibilities and Dilemmas for International NGOs*, Burma Center Netherlands and Transnational Institute, Silkworm Books, Chiang Mai, Thailand, pp.69–109

Robinson, Mark (1992) 'NGOs and Rural Poverty Alleviation: Implications for Scaling-up' in Edwards and Hulme *Making A Difference....*

Save the Children UK (1998) *Indigenous Development Programmes in Myanmar: A Preliminary Survey of Buddhist and Christian Social Initiatives*, unpublished, Yangon, Myanmar

Smillie, Ian and Hailey, John (2001), *Managing for Change*, Earthscan Publications Ltd., London

Smith, Martin (1999a) *Burma: Insurgency and the Politics of Ethnicity*, Zed Books, London

– (2003) 'Burma, The Karen Conflict', in Rudolph, Joseph R. Jr. *Encyclopedia of Modern Ethnic Conflicts*, Greenwood Press, Westport, Connecticut, US, pp.9–25

Smith, Martin (1999b) 'Ethnic Conflict and the Challenge of Civil Society in Burma', in *Strengthening Civil Society in Burma, Possibilities and Dilemmas for International NGOs*, Burma Center Netherlands and Transnational Institute, Silkworm Books, Chiang Mai, Thailand, pp.15–53

Smith, Martin (1996) *Fatal Silence? Freedom of Expression and the Right to Health in Burma*, Article 19

South, Ashley (2005), *Civil Society and the Development of Democracy in Burma*, presentation at Roger Bolton Human Rights, Stockholm, May 2005

Starr, S Frederick (1999) 'Civil Society in Central Asia' in Ruffin, M Holt and Waugh, Daniel C *Civil Society in Central Asia*, University of Washington Press, Seattle, US, pp.27–33

Steinberg, David I (1981) *Burma's Road Toward Development, Growth and Ideology Under Military Rule*, Westview Press, Boulder, Colorado, U.S.

Steinberg, David I (2001) *Burma, The State of Myanmar*, Georgetown University Press, Washington, DC, US

Steinberg, David I (1999) 'A Void in Myanmar: Civil Society in Burma', in *Strengthening Civil Society in Burma, Possibilities and Dilemmas for International NGOs*, Burma Center Netherlands and Transnational Institute, Silkworm Books, Chiang Mai, Thailand, pp.1–14

Tandon, Rajesh and Mohanty, Ranjita (2003) *Does Civil Society Matter? Governance in Contemporary India*, Sage Publications, New Delhi

UNDP (2000) Human Development Report, Oxford University Press, New York

– (2001) Human Development Report, Oxford University Press, New York

UNICEF (2001) *Children and Women in Myanmar: Situation Assessment and Analysis*, Yangon, Myanmar

UNICEF (2000) *National and International NGOs in Myanmar*, Yangon, Myanmar

Uphoff, Norman (1995) 'Why NGOs Are Not a Third Sector: A Sectoral Analysis with Some Thoughts on Accountability, Sustainability and Evaluation', in Edwards, Michael and Hulme, David (eds) *Non-Governmental Organisations Performance and Accountability: Beyond the Magic Bullet*, Earthscan, London, pp.17–30

Zoe, Lu (1996) *Myanmar Proverbs,* Ava House, Yangon, Myanmar

A Annexure

Research Methodology

This research was conducted in 2003 and 2004. The two main surveys (NGOs and CBOs) were conducted over a period of about eight months, from April to November 2003. The research included a literature review on civil society and related issues in Myanmar. Very little relevant information was found, whether from sources inside or outside Myanmar. Focus group discussions were conducted with international and national NGOs, and several interviews were held with donors, international and local NGOs, government officials, UN agencies, historians and other researchers. Finally, a five-person research team conducted two surveys: a survey of NGOs and a survey of CBOs. A third survey, focusing on poor households, was conducted with field staff of Save the Children UK. A fourth survey, focusing on UN agencies, was conducted and analysed separately by the author, due to the small number of agencies. All data entry and analysis from the three main surveys were performed in Microsoft Access. The researchers categorised all open questions and coded all questionnaires, checked forms before date entry, and data were checked after entry as well.

NGO Survey

For this survey, all known and eligible NGOs with offices in Yangon were contacted. The goal was to reach 100% of all eligible NGOs. Many sources were requested to assist in identifying eligible NGOs, including staff of NGOs, international NGOs and UN agencies. This process helped the team significantly increase the list of known NGOs. This survey included 64 national NGOs. Nine NGOs refused to participate and one NGO could not be found. None of these NGOs is large in size and scope of work, nor are they among the better known NGOs. As explained in the text, having an office in Yangon was one of the selection criteria for inclusion in the survey. Therefore, the survey does not represent NGOs based in other parts of the country. The survey was pre-tested in May. More than half of the questions were open-ended which made subsequent analysis a challenge, but which yielded very rich information.

CBO Survey

The CBO Survey was conducted in 140 communities (114 villages and 26 urban wards); there are a total of 67,696 communities in Myanmar, or 65,148 villages and 2,548 urban wards, which therefore puts the urban:rural ratio of the survey at 1:4, compared to that for the nation as a whole (1:25).[1] Ten communities were surveyed in each of 14 townships (out of a total of 324 townships in Myanmar), with one township per each of the 14 states and divisions of Myanmar.

In order to select 14 townships, the research team applied a two-pronged approach. In ten of the 14 states and divisions the research included in the sampling frame all townships considered reasonably secure and accessible (within one day by road, water or air). With the list of townships and the estimated population of each township included in the sampling frame, the team used a PPS (Probability Proportional to Size) sampling method for selecting one township in each of the 10 states and divisions.

The team used purposive sampling in the remaining four states. Two states, Kayah and Kayin, were considered to have major security risks, so the team selected in each state the township deemed the safest. Chin state was considered to have particularly daunting access challenges: road access was the only realistic access, and road conditions were poor or very poor in almost all parts of Chin State. For that state, the team chose the township with easiest access. Finally, for Rakhine State, the team decided to pre-select a particular township to ensure inclusion of one of Myanmar's major ethnic and religious group (ethnic Rohingyas, predominantly Muslim).

To determine the 140 villages of the survey, the team worked from a list provided by the central government which, because it was not completely reliable, had to be supplemented with additional research by the team in the 14 selected townships to verify accuracy. A list of secure and accessible villages in 13 townships was then compiled, from which a random sample of 10 villages per township was determined (there were only 10 secure villages in Loikaw township, in Kayah State, therefore all these villages were included).

In summary, out of 324 townships in Myanmar, 281 townships (87%) were included in the sampling frame, while 43 were excluded. Out of 67,696 villages and wards in Myanmar (MOHA 2001), 7,942 villages and wards (12%) were excluded from the sampling frame. Among the total of 2,992 villages in the 14 selected townships, 1,711 villages (57%) were included in the sampling frame and 1,281 were excluded. Obviously, insecure and more remote communities are under-represented in this survey.

The questionnaire was translated from English into Myanmar language and pre-tested in one township near Yangon in May 2003. As with the NGO survey, about half of the questions were open. Later analysis revealed problems with comprehension by CBOs for a few questions – these are noted in the text.

Upon arrival in each township, the responsible researcher hired four enumerators and conducted a two-day training with them. The researchers identified the enumerators while awaiting township level approval for the survey. The researchers avoided recruiting enumerators chosen or suggested by any township authorities. They made the selection independently, using only five basic criteria: local resident, speak local languages/dialects, minimum 10th standard graduation, good Myanmar literacy skills and good communication skills.

To select CBOs to interview, village leaders or key informants were asked to supply a list of all CBOs in the community, as well as basic information about the village (including population, economic activity, and so on). This list was checked against the criteria defining a CBO for the purposes of this research (see the CBO Chapter). Up to a maximum of five CBOs were selected for interview (if more than five CBOs existed, a simple random sampling process was used to select five). Research teams then met with representatives from the CBOs, ideally two people, one of whom was usually the CBO leader. On average, one village was visited per day. No villages refused to participate in the survey. However, two villages in Pale Township in Sagaing Division had no CBOs. Therefore, the researchers chose two more villages to complete the ten sample villages in each township surveyed. In all, in the 140 villages surveyed, the researchers found a total of 1,284 organisations, with 682 meeting the research criteria[2] (see the Table below). Of these, due to the team being constrained to interview a maximum of five CBOs per village, 455 CBOs were surveyed in depth.

Number of CBOs meeting the Research Criteria in each Township

State/Division Name	Township Name	Number of CBOs	Avg. No. of CBOs/ Community
Chin State	Tiddim	108	11
Kachin State	Myitkyina	82	8
Yangon Division	Insein	82	8
Mon State	Thaton	58	6
Magway Division	Pwintbyu	54	5
Kayin State	Hpa-an	51	5
Kayah State	Loikaw	50	5
Tanintharyi Division	Dawei	47	5
Mandalay Division	Myit-tha	32	3
Shan State	Taung Gyi	28	3
Rakhine State	Bu Thi Taung	27	3
Ayeyarwady Division	Kyaiklat	27	3
Bago Division	Kyauktaga	20	2
Sagaing Division	Pale	16	2
	Total CBOs:	682	Average: 5

Note: The average number of CBOs per community refers to both rural villages and urban wards combined.

There was a large range in village/ward size. Ten of the communities had fewer than 200 people, while four of the communities had more than 10,000 people. The largest cluster of population was in the ranges of 200–399, 400–599 and 600–799, which combined included 47% of the surveyed villages. Agriculture was cited most frequently as the main livelihood occupation (48%, in 14% of villages, it was the only occupation cited), followed by casual labour (41%). The urban bias of the survey is apparent, as national figures indicate that about 57% of the population is involved in agriculture (Department of Labour 2002).

The ethnic majority Bamar (the common term used to refer to the major ethnic group) were well represented in the survey, found in more than half of the surveyed villages. A fair number of villages had Indian, Chin, Kayin and Kachin ethnicities. Unfortunately, the Shan, Rakhine, Mon and Kayah ethnicities were barely represented. In fact, the Mon were not the majority population in any of the surveyed villages or wards. However, it was never the intent of the researchers to include a mix of ethnicities that was equivalent to national ratios.

Poverty Survey

Field staff of Save the Children UK conducted a separate survey of poorest households in 188 villages, aiming to gather and reflect the perspective of the very poorest people in Myanmar towards CBOs. The villages were chosen among villages near the programming area of Save the Children UK. However, villages where Save the Children UK was working or had worked in the past were excluded, to prevent bias. The states and divisions included in this survey were Kayin State, Shan State, Mon State and Ayeyarwady Division. The survey used a simple questionnaire with only closed questions, except for one question in which members of the poorest households were asked to list CBOs.

One household per village was selected, making a total of 188 households interviewed (the most recent government figure on the total number of households in Myanmar was 7,887,620 households, from MOHA 2001). Households were selected in the following way: researchers asked at least two sources in a village where the poorest family lived. If the home of that family was roofed in natural materials (and not tin), an interview was conducted. If not, researchers were required to find another family in the village or move to another village.

Endnotes

1. However, it should be noted that a few of the townships in the CBO survey did not include even one urban ward.

2. Typically, the excluded community organisations were government agencies (e.g. Village Peace and Development Council), legally mandated organisations established specially by the government (e.g., MMCWA and Red Cross), or political organisations (e.g., USDA).

B Annexure

Laws Relevant to NGO Registration

As part of this research, an experienced lawyer was hired to conduct a legal review. The scope of the review included a study of all laws in Myanmar relevant for the registration and operations of local NGOs and CBOs.

1. Organisation of Association Law

This law is applicable to 'a group of persons, in accordance with their own intention, who organise a club, organisation, committee, headquarter and any other association, formed in line with the same objectives'. This law was adopted in 1988; the former Societies Registration Act (1952)– the most common law used previously for NGO registration – was made null and void. The Societies Registration Act was a typical law in former British colonies, patterned after the original Societies Registration Act in India (1861). Organisations registered under the Societies Registration Act shifted their registration under the new Association Law.

Under this law, the Ministry of Home Affairs (MOHA) receives and scrutinises all applications. The entire process can be completed in as little as nine months, but can take as long as 24 months. The first step, as with most laws, is to prepare the organisation document. A MOHA directive sets out a prescribed format with a simple two-page form to be completed by the applicant, listing 11 basic information items such as name, establishment date and address of the association, objectives and workplan, activities, list of executive members and financial statement. This document must be submitted to the Township Peace and Development Council (TPDC) within 30 days of formation. Following the submission, MOHA will scrutinise the association. The scrutiny occurs at every level of administration, from township to district to state/division and, finally, at national level. The steps for registering under this law are summarised in the table below, as are the steps for registering under the other three laws discussed below.

Summary of Steps for Legal Registration

	Association Law	Partnership Act	Cooperative Law	Civil Procedure Code
Step 1	Write 'scheme'	Prepare 'Partnership Deed'	Draft by-laws with guidance, approval of Cooperative Departments at different levels	Write 'scheme' (draft)
Step 2	Submit application to TPDC	Signing ceremony among partners	Seek approval from Cooperative	Seek consent, approval from Attorney
Step 3	MOHA scrutinises	Register 'Partnership Deed' with Office of Registration of Deeds	N/A	File application in competent court
Step 4	Issue legal registration	N/A	N/A	Notice for objection
Step 5	N/A	N/A	N/A	Hearing
Step 6	N/A	N/A	N/A	Order approving the scheme
Estimated time	9–24	45 days months	6–18 months	18 months

Organisations exempted from registering under this law are associations organised for the sole purpose of religious affairs or for business trading, any association organised in compliance with another law and any political party registered or preparing to register with the Multi-party Democracy General Election Commission. These organisations are presumed to be registered under other relevant laws, and, therefore, do not need to register again under this law. Lawful political parties and any organisation with a relationship with any political party are barred from being recognised as associations, as are unlawful organisations, which include any organisation that 'jeopardises the stability of the state and progress of the nation', or that 'jeopardises the smooth function of the state management affairs'. Violations are punishable with up to five years imprisonment.

This law is the most relevant for NGOs, as the intention is to facilitate formation of groups such as associations. Although for-profit organisations can register according to this law, the law is aimed at non-profit organisations.

2. Partnership Act

The Partnership Act allows any number of partners to form a partnership for any legal purpose agreed among the partners and stated in their jointly signed deed. The partners have some flexibility to determine voting rights and decision-making procedures, within limitations. However, any major decisions, such as a change of business, must be unanimously agreed. All partners have unlimited liability. Partners can run any type of business, whether for profit or non-profit. The government does not interfere with partnerships, as long as their activities do not violate any other laws and they do not require intervention.

3. Cooperative Society Law

A primary Cooperative Society may be established with at least five people who decide to collectively promote their interests. A Cooperative Syndicate may be formed with at least three primary Cooperative Societies. A Union of Cooperative Syndicates may be formed with any number of syndicates, and a Central Cooperative Society may be formed with any number of unions. A Cooperative Society cannot carry out any activities until it has been registered through the Department of Cooperatives under the Ministry of Cooperatives.

Cooperatives have a long and complex history in Myanmar. During the Burma Socialist Party Programme era (1962–88), cooperatives were formed in villages throughout the country, often without the consent of farmers. Though farmers traditionally worked cooperatively (sharing labour and providing mutual support), the official cooperatives imposed many restrictions and requirements that stifled initiative and led to substantial financial losses (see Steinberg 2001). Following the change in government in 1988, most cooperatives dissolved.

The government has recently launched attempts to revive cooperatives. They are promoting them through mass media and through other means to encourage farmers and businesses to join them. The approach this time, unlike in the 1960s and 1970s, appears to be promoting voluntary participation, not mandatory participation.

4. Code of Civil Procedure

Any trust forming for public or charitable purposes may register under this code. Two or more persons, with the consent of the Attorney General or an officer appointed by the state, may apply through a competent court. The application includes the objectives, a list of management committee members, the duties and responsibilities of the trustees, accounting and auditing procedures, annual meetings and other procedures. The court has the power to remove any trustee and appoint a new one, turning over the property of the trustee who was removed. The court has a wide discretion regarding administration of public trusts. The court is entitled to take into consideration not only the wishes of the founder, to the extent they can be known, but also the past history of the institution and the way in which it was managed.

Each of the four laws described earlier has many advantages and disadvantages. The Table below summarises these. Overall, for speed and convenience, the Partnership Act would appear to have the most advantages. However, it would not have the most relevance for NGOs' type of work. For relevance to NGOs' social work as a non-profit organisation, the Organisation of Association Law would appear to have the most advantages. However, the waiting and the procedures can be cumbersome. For cooperative efforts, the Cooperative Society Law would have the most advantages. However, the previous history of cooperatives in Myanmar has discouraged some people from joining such efforts. For matching the objectives of an NGO, the Code of Civil Procedure would have some advantages. However, the procedures for registering can be very complicated and costly.

Advantages and Disadvantages of Each Law

	Advantages	Disadvantages
Association Law	– Best matches non-profit objectives – NGOs can function independently	– Possibly lengthy wait – Involvement of layers of bureaucracy – Uncertainty of approval
Partnership Act	– Procedure simple and quick – No waiting after members decide – Partnership can function independently – Establishment is certain; registration most certain	– May not fit NGO purposes – Unlimited liability – May need a lawyer to register – Objectives must be transparent – Clear delegation needed
Cooperative Law	– Matches NGO purposes – Cooperatives can help increase production	– Approval dependant on layers, possibly long wait – Government directly oversees – Myanmar people had previous negative experiences – Better suited for production than NGO work
Civil Procedure Code	– Matches NGO purposes – NGOs can function somewhat independently	– Requires lawyer – Procedure complicated and lengthy – Costs may be high

Many other laws apply indirectly to NGOs' operations, relating to publication, speech, banking, among others. One particular law that applies to certain NGOs is the Protection of Public Property Law (1963). NGOs that use public property operate under this law. Three of the surveyed NGOs were using public property for their institutions.

Because of the large number of religious organisations operating in Myanmar, it is useful to know that Buddhist monks were governed by the Law Relating to the Sangha Organisation, 1990. The focus of this law is the 'purification, perpetuation and propagation of the Sasana (Buddhist religion)'. This is the only law relating to activities of monks. None of the other four laws mentioned previously would apply to monks seeking to form an organisation. Under this law, monks can form an organisation and function with the unwritten consent of the Sangha Organisation, as long as their activities are discreet and welfare-oriented. Often monks initiate activities without forming any sort of organisation. Although these would therefore not be specifically covered by the Sangha law, these activities will be tolerated if the local authorities feel they do not violate Buddhist practices or cause threats to the government's authority or disturbances among the people.

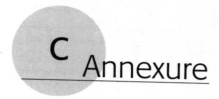

Annexure

Basic NGO Information

Mission Statements and Primary Beneficiaries of Surveyed NGOs

Name of NGO	Vision/Mission or Main Goals	Primary Beneficiaries
All Myanmar Hindu Central Board	To propagate fundamental teachings of Hinduism; to protect and promote the religious interests of all sects and creeds within Hinduism as well as the Religious places, temples and cremation grounds in Myanmar; to provide assistance for the social welfare, education and health of the Hindu community	All Hindus as well as other religious communities
All Myanmar Tamil Hindu Foundation (H.Q.)	To promote the life of Tamil Hindus living in Myanmar by providing social welfare assistance	All Tamil Hindus living in Myanmar especially the marginalised
Asho Chin Baptist Conference	To spread the Gospel of Jesus Christ and labour for the ministry and growth of the church	Asho Chin Baptist believers and the needy communities

Name of NGO	Vision/Mission or Main Goals	Primary Beneficiaries
Catholic Bishops Conference of Myanmar	A Christ-centred family participating in loving and serving God and people of all faiths and cultures, ever responding to the signs of the times	The whole Catholic Church
Dhamma Theikdhi Monastic Education School	To provide care and protection as well as education to orphans, impoverished children, children who cannot afford an education	Orphans, street children, impoverished children and people connected in some way to those children
Dhammaythaka Parahita Nunnery School	To enable young Buddhist nuns to become graduates, to become educated	All young nuns poor or rich irrespective of race and nationality
Eden Handicap Service Centre	To provide a better environment where children with physical and mental handicap could experience love, quality care and compassion so that they could feel and see the positive side of life. We hope we can help them regain their self-esteem.	Under 18 physically and mentally handicapped children
Forest Resource Environment Development and Conservation Association (FREDA)	Contributing to the conservation of forests, soil, and water resources as well as to the development of rural areas will lead to prevention of soil erosion and floods, regular seasons and weather, and a higher living standard of the rural population	The rural population (public) are the beneficiaries. Scientists in fields related to environment or ecology will also benefit in carrying out research activities
Funeral Help Organisation	To provide funeral services free of charge	Those who have passed away and the bereaved families, dead bodies without kith and kin
Grace Home	For the homeless orphans to acquire an education and be able to stand on their own feet; to demonstrate that orphans can become valuable young people if they are provided support and are cultivated	Orphans, homeless children, abandoned children, and children rejected by society

Name of NGO	Vision/Mission or Main Goals	Primary Beneficiaries
Guru Nanak Free Dispensary and Eye Hospital	To provide medical treatment to those in poverty regardless of race and religious belief	Those who come for medical treatment regardless of race and religion
Hman Kinn Monastic Education School	To prevent conversions to other religions and their spreading; for the Buddhist religion and teachings to last long; to create educational opportunities for orphans and poor children	Orphans, street children, impoverished children and people connected in some way to those children
Hninzigone Home for the Aged	To render all help to the aged persons who come here for refuge, with the provision of free food, clothing, accommodation, medical care, a good social environment conducive to self-contemplation, merit-making and attainment of peace of mind	Donors get merit of their contribution; aged residents (Bos, Bwas) get merit to perform meritorious deeds
Jivitadana Sangha Hospital	To provide free medical services to all needy persons irrespective of class, creed, colour, sex or age	All those who need medical treatment irrespective of class, race and religion
Kachin Baptist Convention	By speaking the Truth in a Spirit of Love, we must grow up in every way to Christ, who is the head	All the Kachin Baptist believers and some project area communities include non-Christian and other denominations
Karuna Myanmar Social Services	Toward tranquillity and development for all human beings	The community
Kayin Baptist Convention	To spread the Gospel of Christ in Myanmar and in other countries as well	Members; poor, the needy
Law Kahta Cariya Foundation	With sympathy will beautify the world	The poor
Little Sisters of the Poor Home for the Aged Poor	To provide protection and care with earnest goodwill to elderly persons who genuinely have no one to turn to regardless of race and religion; to enable the elderly persons to engage in their respective religious practices in peace and quiet to prepare themselves for the transition to the next life	Elderly persons without anyone to turn to

Name of NGO	Vision/Mission or Main goals	Primary Beneficiaries
Madarsah Majidia Hifzul Quraan and Orphanage	To enable Muslim children to memorise the religious text	Muslim children who are orphans
Mary Chapman School for the Deaf	To expand the school and offer all the courses required to complete middle school	Deaf Children
Metta Development Foundation	The aim is to bring about sustained development and prosperity to indigenous ethnic groups' regions, where there has been little development due to civil war	The local communities
Mingalar Byu-har Welfare Association	Enlightened by the brilliance of the thirty eight guidelines of the Mangalar Sutta we should convey to all the inhabitants of this world the message of lasting peace, well being and unity; we shall extend our good deeds, help and protection towards all living beings. We shall support, care for and protect all the poor and miserable people irrespective of race and religion	All those who are in need of support in education, health and social matters regardless of race and religion. All the donors will get the merit of their Dhama (Charity)
Muslim Free Hospital and Medical Relief Society	To help the poor, the needy and the rich without discrimination of class creed or colour	The poor and needy sick of all communities without discrimination of class, creed or colour
Muslim Women's Home for the Aged	To offer shelter and care to Muslim elderly women whose families cannot afford to look after them; to provide physical, mental, moral and social support	Muslim elderly women
Myanmar Anti-Narcotics Association	While the Myanmar government is fighting the scourge of narcotic drugs in Myanmar as a national movement, the association will contribute to the government effort and provide support; as the rapid spread of AIDS among Intravenous Drug Users has necessitated urgent immediate all-round concerted efforts for effective prevention and protection, the association will contribute to this effort	All the citizens of the country

Name of NGO	Vision/Mission or Main Goals	Primary Beneficiaries
Myanmar Baptist Convention (MBC)	To spread and propagate the gospel of Jesus Christ and labour for the ministry and the growth of the church in Myanmar and throughout the world	All Baptist believers and communities of non-Christian and other denomination
Myanmar Business Coalition on AIDS	To bring corporate resources to assist in HIV/AIDS prevention; to promote non-discriminatory workplace policies and sustained education programmes; to coordinate between the business companies and other government agencies and NGOs involved in HIV/AIDS issues in the workplace	Workers, their families and the community
Myanmar Christian Fellowship of the Blind	To turn them into Differently Abled Persons	The blind
Myanmar Christian Health Workers' Services Association	For everyone to enjoy a richer lifetime 'I am come that they might have life ... more abundantly'.	The public
Myanmar Christian Leprosy Mission	To serve persons affected by leprosy (PALs)	PALs and their families
Myanmar Council of Churches	To unify all the Christian Churches in Myanmar; to have better understanding and friendship among the Churches; to have mutual confidence and recognition of one another's practices among Churches; to cooperate in Church affairs where coordination and cooperation are appropriate; to work toward the ultimate goal of having a unified Church	Members, Churches
Myanmar Health Assistant Association	Friendship among health assistants; effective coordination of health care delivery; enhancing further development of intellectual and technical skills of health assistants	Rural population that make up 75% of the total population

Name of NGO	Vision/Mission or Main Goals	Primary Beneficiaries
Myanmar Literacy Resource Centre	To transform Myanmar into a learning society and develop human resources through non-formal literacy activities; to promote education standard of the country	Illiterate and newly literate persons
Myanmar Nurses Association (Centre)	The Association aims to carry out organising activities in accordance with the health policies laid down by the State in order that all the nurses become actively involved in health care activities; to provide support to raise the social, educational and professional standards of nurses; and to participate with unity in cases of national emergencies and requirements	The public including the grassroots levels
Myanmar Women Entrepreneurs' Association	To organise the energies and enterprise of the Myanmar women into a sisterhood with awareness and mission for social and self-development and with national and international focus and vision.	Myanmar women entrepreneurs as well as marginalised women
Myanmar Women's Development Association	To utilise women's physical and intellectual powers in national development activities; to accept and cultivate socially underdeveloped women belonging to nationalities living in border areas based on national unity regardless of race or religious belief. To protect and cultivate women without parents, relatives or guardians, women whose parents, relatives and guardians are so socially deprived as to send them to the Association, and homeless women; to promote the morality of women under the care of the Association, their basic education, and acquisition of vocational skills for their livelihood	Young women under the care of the Association

Name of NGO	Vision/Mission or Main Goals	Primary Beneficiaries
Myanmar Young Crusaders	To improve the morality of the young drug addicts; to provide care to orphans; to teach the Bible to drug addicts and other young people; to enable leprosy patients to have treatment and find employment; to expand Bible societies and construct churches; to continue the activities of the late Rev. Dr. David Yone Mo	Lepers, orphans, drug abusers, young people who would like to have Bible training
Myitta Wadi Parahita Monastic Education School	For the poor children to acquire an education and be able to stand on their own feet; to demonstrate that poor children can become valuable young people in their community if they are provided support and are cultivated.	Poor children of different races especially from Chin and Shan States
Nan Oo Education and Parahita School	Buddha's teachings must spread and reach to remote areas of Myanmar through educating young nationalities	Impoverished children and orphans
Ngapaw Kyunn Nunnery School	To enable poor and orphanage girls to become graduates, to become educated	Orphans and poor girls and young women
Patauk Shwewar Monastic Primary School	To provide care and protection as well as education to impoverished children, children who cannot afford an education	Impoverished children, orphans, abandoned children and people connected in some way to those children
Pwo Kayin Baptist Conference	To spread the Gospel of Jesus Christ and labour for the ministry and growth of the church	Church members and the needy communities
Pyinnya Tazaung Association	Publication of the monthly Pyinnya Tazaung Magazine for the capacity building of the teachers in the country	Primary school teachers and students as well as all education staff
Sasana Yetkhita Buddhist Missionary Monastic Primary School	Teaching of Buddhist texts, actual practice of Buddha's teachings and organisation of pilgrimage trips in order to bring about the following: to prevent conversions to other religions and their spreading;	Orphans, street children, abandoned children and people connected in some way to those children

Name of NGO	Vision/Mission or Main Goals	Primary Beneficiaries
	to prevent marriages with members of other religions when the children grow up; for the Buddhist religion and teachings to last long	
Shalom Foundation (Nyein Foundation)	The vision is to support the process of building a stable and just society based on mutual understanding and respect of diverse cultures, customs and traditions leading to sustainable peace and to sustainable and participatory development of communities, society and the nation as a whole	Community Organisations and Religious Organisations; grassroots communities; youth and women; persons actively engaged in peace keeping and development work
Shwe Pyi Hein Free Health Services-on-Wheels	Doctors and nurses go by car taking with them health equipment and medicines to provide treatment in the homes of people especially the impoverished. It is free health services-on-wheels	People who are impoverished, who need assistance for health matters, who have come to Yangon for medical treatment
Tezeindar Rama National Races Parahita School	To provide care and protection as well as education to orphans, impoverished children, children who cannot afford an education from all over Myanmar	Impoverished children and orphans
The Myanmar Medical Association	To promote and advance the science of medicine; to promote continuing medical education and medical research among the medical profession; to promote cooperation and foster a fraternal spirit among its members; to safeguard the honour and dignity of the medical profession; to maintain a high ethical standard among the medical profession	The general public and medical doctors
The Salvation Army, Myanmar Region	Its mission is to preach the gospel of Jesus Christ and meet human needs in His name without discrimination	Everyone regardless of race or religious belief; the impoverished; orphans; those Living with HIV; the community

Name of NGO	Vision/Mission or Main Goals	Primary Beneficiaries
Thonehtat Parahita Monastic Education School	To provide a happy environment for primary to high school education to impoverished children and those who cannot otherwise have an education for various reasons	Impoverished children who cannot afford an education
U Hla Tun Hospice (Cancer) Foundation	The hospice provides free care for patients who are poor or have no family support.	Impoverished cancer patients who have no one to turn to or benefit from
Wai-Neya Sukha Drinking Water Association	To provide drinking water for the people at pagodas, monasteries and other places alive with turning crowds in Yangon and districts; on the festival day of Shwe Dagon Pagoda and on other days of religious significance, the association offers ice-cold drinking water to all pilgrims; to construct and donate facilities of stands for drinking water elsewhere	All pilgrims to pagodas, visitors to monasteries and all people in need of drinking water and water for domestic use
Yadana Beikman Parahita Monastic Education School	To provide a happy environment for primary to high school education to impoverished children from different states and divisions	Impoverished children who cannot afford an education
Yadanapon Yeik Nyein	To enable children to become educated, to pass the tenth standard and to become graduates	Orphans and impoverished children
Yangon Kayin Baptist Women Association	To stand for the all-round development of women, physically and spiritually	Women
Yinthway Foundation	Supporting child development in communities	Parents and pre-school children
Young Men's Buddhist Association (YMBA)	Development and Propagation of nationality, language, religion and education	Buddhist young people
Young Men's Christian Association Yangon	The YMCA works for equal opportunities and justice for everyone; the YMCA promotes loving kindness and understanding in social	Young people; people facing difficulties and the handicapped; those facing natural disasters

Name of NGO	Vision/Mission or Main Goals	Primary Beneficiaries
Young Men's Christian Associations (National Council)	dealings; the YMCA works to create conditions for integrity, profound thinking, and innovation in the association and in the community; the YMCA will always make best use of deep past experiences of Christians in leading the work programme; the YMCA works for development using the overall development pattern	
Young Women's Christian Association (National)	Physical, mental and spiritual development in young men To empower women to attain their full potentials before God; 'Train a woman – Build a Nation'.	Young people, rural population and the poor All women regardless of race, religious belief and social status

Note: The mission statement for the Shwe Thanlwin Home for the Aged was not available. Two NGOs declined to be identified.

Year of Formation and NGO Age (as at 2003)

	Name of Myanmar NGOs	Year	Age
1	Myanmar Baptist Convention (MBC)	1865	138
2	Young Men's Christian Association Yangon	1894	109
3	Yangon Kayin Baptist Women Association	1895	108
4	Little Sisters of the Poor Home for the Aged Poor	1898	105
5	Young Women's Christian Association (National)	1900	103
6	Young Men's Buddhist Association (YMBA)	1906	97
7	Kachin Baptist Convention	1910	93
8	Pwo Kayin Baptist Conference	1910	93
9	Kayin Baptist Convention	1913	90
10	The Myanmar Council of Churches	1914	89
11	Wai-Naya Sukha Drinking Water Association	1914	89
12	The Salvation Army - Myanmar Region	1915	88

13	Mary Chapman School for the Deaf	1920	83
14	Asho Chin Baptist Conference	1924	79
15	The Myanmar Medical Association	1926	77
16	Muslim Free Hosptial And Medical Relief Society	1937	66
17	Jivitadana Sangha Hospital	1940	63
18	Hninzigone Home for the Aged	1943	60
19	Myanmar Women's Development Association	1947	56
20	Myanmar Nurses Association (Centre)	1948	55
21	Madarsah Majidia Hifzul Quraan and Orphanage	1950	53
22	National Council of Young Men's Christian Associations	1951	52
23	Pyiññya Tazaung Association (Light of Education)	1952	51
24	All-Myanmar Hindu Federation (Centre)	1953	50
25	Catholic Bishops Conference of Myanmar	1954	49
26	Guru Nanak Free Dispensary and Eye Hospital	1956	47
27	Patack Shwewar Monastic Primary School	1958	45
28	Nan Oo Education and Parahita School	1958	45
29	Tezeindarrama National Races Parahita School	1962	41
30	Myanmar Young Crusaders	1974	29
31	Myanmar Christian Fellowship of the Blind	1975	28
32	Sasana Rakkhita Buddhist Missionary Monastic Primary School	1979	24
33	Myitta Wadi Parahita Monastic Education School	1980	23
34	Myanmar Christian Leprosy Mission	1984	19
35	Muslim Women's Home for the Aged	1989	14
36	Dhamma Theikdhi Monastic Education School	1991	12
37	Yadanapon Yeik Nyein	1992	11
38	Ngapyaw Kyun Nunnery School	1992	11

39	Myanmar Christian Health Workers' Services Association	1992	11
40	Hman Kinn Monastic Education School	1993	10
41	Myanmar Health Assistant Association	1994	9
42	Myanmar Anti-Narcotics Association	1994	9
43	Myanmar women Entrepreneurs' Association	1995	8
44	Karuna Myanmar Social Services	1996	7
45	Forest Resource Environment Development and Conservation Association (FREDA)	1996	7
46	Yinthway Foundation	1997	6
47	Grace Home (Orphanage)	1997	6
48	Dhammaythaka Parahita Nunnery School	1997	6
49	Mingalar Byu-har Welfare Association	1997	6
50	U Hla Tun Hospice (Cancer) Foundation	1998	5
51	Metta Development Foundation	1998	5
52	Myanmar Literacy Resource Centre	1999	4
53	Shwe Thanlwin Home for the Aged	1999	4
54	Eden Handicap Service Centre	2000	3
55	Funeral Help Organisation	2000	3
56	Shalom Foundation (Nyein Foundation)	2000	3
57	Yadana Beikman Parahita Monastic Education School	2000	3
58	Law Kahta Cariya Foundation	2001	2
59	All Myanmar Tamil Hindu Foundation	2001	2
60	Shwe Pyi Hein Free Health Services-on-Wheels	2002	1
61	Three-Storey Parahita Monastic Education School	2002	1
62	Myanmar Business Coalition on AIDS	2002	1

D Annexure

Brief Descriptions of the Myanmar Maternal and Child Welfare Association and the Myanmar Red Cross

Myanmar Maternal & Child Welfare Association (MMCWA)

Established: Vision/Mission: Main goals:	30th of April 1991. Improved quality of the life of the people • To disseminate health information through information, education and communication (IEC) programmes nationwide. • To plan, implement and monitor programmes on maternal and child health (MCH) including reproductive health to reach the community at grass roots level. • To establish Child Day Care Centres to facilitate early childhood development and also enable mothers to work and earn family income. • To provide scholarships, to enable children to enrol, remain in school and complete primary, middle and high school education. • To plan and implement functional literacy programmes focusing on the

Main Activities:	needs of the rural community. ● To plan, implement and evaluate income generation programmes including skills training and micro credit schemes, for women and girls from low-income families. ● Health education, production and dissemination of IEC materials ● Establishment of Maternity Homes to provide maternal and child health care ● Expansion of Reproductive Health and Adolescent Reproductive Health programmes including HIV/AIDS. ● Promotion of nutritional status of under 5 years children by means of health education on nutrition, growth monitoring, provision of supplementary lunch and cooking demonstration. ● Provision of child day care centres for early childhood development and to enable mothers to work. ● Provision of financial assistance, to students to enable them to remain in school. ● Functional literacy programmes for children as well as adults. ● Income generation programmes with provision of skills training, loans and supplies. ● Care of the elderly. ● Corrective surgery for congenital defects. ● Establishment of model village for rural development. ● Cooperation and collaboration with other organisations.
Primary Beneficiaries:	Communities, mostly mothers and children

Myanmar Red Cross Society

Established:	The society came into existence as a branch of the Indian Red Cross Society in 1920. When Burma was politically separated from India in 1937, it was recognised as the Burma Red Cross Society.
Vision:	To be the leading community based humanitarian organisation throughout Myanmar acting with and for the most vulnerable at all times
Mission:	Through its nation wide network of volunteers, the Myanmar Red Cross Society will work to promote a healthier and safer environment for the people of Myanmar giving priority to the most vulnerable communities and individuals. In times of distress and disaster, the Myanmar Red Cross Society will assist those affected and help them return to normal life
Main Goal:	To prevent and alleviate human suffering
Main Activities:	• Health promotion • Preventive means • Disaster preparedness and response
Primary Beneficiaries:	The community

E Annexure

Detailed list of CBO Beneficiaries (as defined by CBOs)

In the table, categories are marked with C, O, R, M, R+ and M+, which correspond to: C=community, O=other, R=religious denomination-based, M=membership-based, R=religious denomination-based, but other beneficiaries also assisted, M= membership-based but non-members also assisted. These super-categories correspond to those in Table 15 in the text.

Primary Beneficiaries	Religious	Social Affairs	PTA	Health, Water and Sanitation	Agriculture CBOs	Other CBOs	Total	
People in the community, in the village; all the households in the village. C	54	60	4	6		8	132	29%
School children. C		2	98	1			101	22%
People who have the religion, those who share a religious faith. R	71	2				1	74	16%

Member households in the village, members of the organisation or group. M	22	11			8	2	43	9%
Members of the Sangha (Order of Buddhist monks), Sangha within the village. R	18						18	4%
Poor people in the village, the impoverished. C	1	2	2			4	9	2%
Members of the Sangha (Order of Buddhist monks), Sangha within the village + People in the community, in the village; all the households in the village. R+	8	1					9	2%
Everyone regardless of religion. C	8						8	2%
People in the community, in the village; all the households in the village + Member households in the village, members of the organisation or group. M+	2	6					8	2%
Those who do meritorious deeds; well-wishers; donors. R	6	1					7	2%
Children from poor families. C	3 .		3				6	1%

People who have the religion, those who share a religious faith + People in the community, in the village; all the households in the village. R+	5	1					6	1%
Orphans. C	2	2					4	1%
Members of the Sangha (Order of Buddhist monks), Sangha within the village + People who have the religion, those who share a religious faith. R	4						4	1%
People in the community, in the village; all the households in the village + Poor people in the village, the impoverished. C	2	1					3	1%
Members of the Sangha (Order of Buddhist monks), Sangha within the village + Children from poor families. R+	3						3	1%
Orphans + Children from poor families. C	1	1	1				3	1%
People of the same nationality (Kayins, Pa-Os). O						2	2	0%
People who have the religion, those who share a religious faith + Children from poor families. R+	2						2	0%

Those who recite prayers + People in the community, in the village; all the households in the village. R+	2						2	0%
Member households in the village, members of the organisation or group + Poor people in the village, the impoverished. M+		2					2	0%
Elderly people who are poor and have no one and nowhere to turn to + Orphans.C	1	1					2	0%
Returnees from the other country who didn't find good employment there. O						1	1	0%
Members of the Sangha (Order of Buddhist monks), Sangha within the village + Member households in the village, members of the organisation or group. M		1					1	0%
People who have the religion, those who share a religious faith + Those who recite prayers. R	1						1	0%
People who have the religion, those who share a religious faith + School children. R+	1						1	0%

People who have the religion, those who share a religious faith + Orphans. R+	1						1	0%
People who have the religion, those who share a religious faith + Those who do meritorious deeds; well-wishers; donors R	1						1	0%
Member households in the village, members of the organisation or group + School children. M+		1					1	0%
Total	219	95	108	7	8	18	455	

F Annexure

Myanmar Population

Myanmar has a total population of about 52 million people. The population is distributed among the country's 14 states and divisions as follows:

Population Distribution by State/Division

State/Division	Population (million)
Kachin State	1.364
Kayah State	0.293
Kayin State	1.575
Chin State	0.495
Mon State	2.672
Rakhine State	2.915
Shan State	5.061
Ayeryarwady Division	7.184
Bago Division	5.327
Magway Division	4.873
Mandalay Division	7.246
Sagaing Division	5.655
Tanintharyi Division	1.455
Yangon Division	6.056
Total	**52 million**

Source: Central Statistics Organisation, 2002